I0415970

IF ONLY IT WAS FICTION

All of the people presented and featured in this work are people I actually knew and lived with every day--if you could call what we did living. Only the name of one individual has been changed, per his request. The politicians are real, and guilty of all of their sins. And I still miss my city.

Katrina and The Lost City of New Orleans
ISBN #1-4116-6366-7

THE LOST CITY

LIZARD LICK, North Carolina, 7 September, 2005

Year after year, those of us scraping to survive in the real Nawlins would watch people breeze into town for conventions or Mardi Gras or JazzFest who would never once think about looking at the city we lived in and loved/hated. Only a few adventurous visitors took in our Museum of Art at City Park in MidCity. If a tourist went to Tipitina's or Vaughn's, we'd damn near give them a medal.

But now, in the aftermath of Hurricane Katrina, people are *finally* getting a look at the real Nawlins--its streets, its abandoned lots, its people without cars or decent jobs or homes--on their television screens and in their newspapers. America claims it is appalled at what it sees after Katrina and that it's surprised to find out what Nawlins has always really been like.

Figure 1: A levee that failed in the Ninth Ward.

It's a little late, though, we think. It's late because that New Orleans is gone, except in the memories of those of us who lived there.

This book is an attempt to share some those memories with you.

In this book, among the things you will learn that you probably didn't know about our lost city of New Orleans:

- One of the largest jails in the United States, holding state, local and federal prisoners was located in the City of New Orleans-and was its third largest (if unacknowledged) industry.

- New Orleans had twice the poverty level of the rest of the United States. In the Ninth Ward (where I lived most of my time in New Orleans), a vast number of people made less than $10,000 a year.

- Known for its voodoo history, its Ghost Tours, its historical architecture, Mardi Gras and JazzFest, New Orleans-- because it was the geopolitical prize of the Louisiana Purchase--is the jewel in the crown of American commerce because the Port of New Orleans is one of the five largest in the world. America's economic predominance requires that there always be a New Orleans.

These are only three of the "astonishing" facts about the real New Orleans that this book will reveal.

A PLACE OF LOVE AND PAIN

You find what you really love and you *know* it is going to hurt you real bad, but you keep coming back. Even after she tries to kill you, you keep coming back. That's what everyone I knew said about New Orleans: you keep coming back.

There was a fantasy New Orleans, as my friend Logan in Rome once said, but there was a real New Orleans, too. I lived there.

I knew a lot of people who lived there and sat on the other side of the bars where I worked--on Bourbon Street, and on Frenchmen Street, which is the place Bourbon Street should have been as far as the locals were concerned. Some of my patrons said I was the best bartender in town. I expected them to say that. I knew they said that to other bartenders on the fringe of the French Quarter and up in the Quarter itself. You'd buy them a drink if they flattered you. That's the New Orleans Way.

But the city I'm writing about doesn't exist anymore. It is gone. New Orleans is no more than a ghost to haunt me, like all the other ghosts of the famous New Orleans Ghost Tours that the tourists used to flock down to see.

New Orleans is the Lost City of America.

New Orleans has disappeared as surely as the lost city of Atlantis or the lost city of Pompeii, which former mayor Marc Morial and Senator Mary Landrieu (D-LA.) have compared us to in their statements.

That New Orleans, the New Orleans I mean to tell you about, that will never, ever, exist again--that city of love, lust, death and sex--will never exist again.

If the Baptists up at the Louisiana state capitol have anything to do with it, they will replace Marie Laveau's city with a damned neutered theme park, sanitized and rated PG.

It will not be the place where I could buy a whore a drink at the end of her night, from where I worked behind the bar, and she knew we were both in the same business.

If those people in the rest of the state have their way, the New Orleans I knew, that place that damn near killed me, will never come back again.

I thought New Orleans had hurt me real bad before I watched her die in front of my face, before I watched the rest of America--let's face it, a country she was never part of anyway--say, "Hey, we'll be there for you a** in a minute."

And then America didn't show up for us.

The President arrived days later for a fly-by. The Secretary of State was in Manhattan buying shoes before attending a Broadway show while little old ladies were dying in attics in the New Orleans I used to love. Some of those little old ladies believed that help was on the way from this country they loved. They were wrong.

And now they are gone.

New Orleans is gone.

The worst part was having to watch it on CNN.

Ten days after the storm, Hurricane Katrina, you still couldn't call anybody with a cell phone in the 504 area code. They could call you, though, if they thought of it and weren't busy trying to deal with not having a home or a job anymore.

Novelist Anne Rice, a New Orleanian, wrote an op-ed for the *New York Times* that was published on 4 September, 2005.It concluded with these words:

> But to my country I want to say this: During this crisis you failed us. You looked down on us; you dismissed our victims; you dismissed us. You want our Jazz Fest, you want our Mardi Gras, you want our cooking and our music. Then when you saw us in real trouble, when you saw a tiny minority preying on the weak among us, you called us "Sin City," and turned your backs.

> Well, we are a lot more than all that. And though we may seem the most exotic, the most atmospheric and, at times, the most downtrodden part of this land, we are still part of it. We are Americans. We are you.

"… the most downtrodden part of this land…"

Ain't it the truth. New Orleans, by my own avowal and that of many, was the American Haiti.

Listen:

Chapter 1

NEW ORLEANS, Dauphine Street - 15 February, 2002

New Orleans is the only city in America where the U.S. Postal Service does not deliver mail on Mardi Gras. I spent the week leading up to Mardi Gras Day on Bourbon Street working (minimum) fourteen hour days. And Mardi Gras, *sans* the krewe parades, on Bourbon Street is... Let's put it this way: imagine a giant frat party in the center of your town, going on for blocks and blocks, except all the businesses welcome it and expect it to make an approximate third of their annual incomes, the way other businesses in America might expect Christmas holiday sales to make a quarter of their annual incomes. So people complain about the rowdy, no inhibitions, out of control ("What the hell are you doing?!? Don't piss in here!") behavior while knowing that their prosperity depends upon it.

And *every* bartender, waitress, and cook on the beat has stories of working 14 to 17 hours straight, from the Wednesday before (sometimes) until the Wednesday after Mardi Gras. It's like carrying an egg as a badge of honor.

 After about three days of the on-going rush of music blaring from the souvenir shops trying to attract customers and from the live bands in the clubs, after all the "Woo-Hoo!" and "Show us your tits!" and "Dude! Look! HUGE ASS BEER TO GO! Let's go get a huge ass beer to go!" "Kewl! Huge Ass Beer!" long days of catering to the amateur drunks and very little sleep, a kind of hallucinatory glaze settles over everything and all of your perceptions.

Exhaustion has been used as a form of torture by most modern armies. Sleep deprivation (dream deprivation) leads to an altered state of consciousness. This, too, is part of the New Orleans Way.

> Purple, Gold, and Green are the Traditional Mardi Gras Colors. Purple represents justice; green, faith; and gold, power. That's the significance of the traditional Mardi Gras colors.

Figure 2: Bourbon Street at night.

If you manage to work less than fourteen hours, you take it as a cause for celebration. You stop at a small local bar halfway between Bourbon Street and home on the path of your walk, and take the opportunity of an extra hour to yourself to continue your paean to the season. You'd expect to find those attributes among Mardi Gras celebrants. To the contrary, you all-too-often find that the people most willing to embrace the New Orleans Way aren't inclined toward any of those qualities. I've taken to saying that the only way to understand something that happens in New Orleans is to correlate the various "versions" of the story that you hear. New Orleans is a city of versions. You find it difficult to run into two people who have the same version of even the most mundane event. So you have to dig for the (usually self-serving) interest which the particular version you're getting is meant to reinforce or promote.

Honor, an essential component of true justice, is something you quickly come not to expect. Power, on the other hand, dictates the

8

> Let me explain the Cop Parade. I'm told it's one of the three Must See events in New Orleans. Mardi Gras is OVER at midnight. Suddenly it's Lent. Ash Wednesday. The New Orleans police march through the French Quarter and kick all the revelers out. The bars close---even on Bourbon Street!!!!---and the locals get to rest.

actions and reactions of both the strong and weak. Those with power wield it brutally; the powerless toady towards their betters. The ritual politeness here is as thick and transparent as you'll find in any Islamic country. "Sir" and "Ma'am" simply replace "Effendi" and "Bey" by dint of geography. As to faith, no one is as pious as the publican and the Pharisee.

LONG PAUSE.

Lundi Gras---the Monday preceding Mardi Gras --comes like an epiphany. It's still show time, but the pressure is strangely off. Your co-workers go out of their way to show their appreciation. They start telling you about places to go and people to meet, and make plans to show you the Cop Parade.

> There is a saying here that you can tell out-of-towners because they wear beads even when it isn't Mardi Gras.

There is reeking camaraderie. You have the sense that you have passed some crucial test. You have already seen the worst if you have completed Lundi Gras and have shown grace under pressure. Mardi Gras Day will be the end of the marathon and you will fall, exhausted into some wonderful embrace. New Orleans has taken you. Everything about you has changed. It is the first day of the rest of your life in New Orleans, you learn from another bartender, who treats you with new respect. He suggests that the two of you get together on his day off. It feels as though you have learned the handshake of some secret society.

Like all euphoria, this one can be short-lived. 2002 was a slow Mardi Gras, one of the slowest in the last five years, everyone tells you. One of the managers in the chain of clubs and restaurants your company owns decides to have the promotional slogan of a beer campaign body-painted on her torso and flash for the crowds like the Quarter's traditional "bead whores." Everyone complains about low sales and low tips. In your position, pumping out Huge Ass Beers in a bar that has been converted to a "beer box" to withstand the damage of crowds, it matters less because you don't get tipped, anyway. The brother holding the HUGE ASS BEER sign near Toulouse tells you that he's making "mad bank" from the street crowds and also being tipped out by the bartenders at other bars, so he's having a great time. This is his first Mardi Gras, too, so he has no idea what mad bank is by Bourbon Street standards. Theories are tossed around like the fake doubloons of the parade krewes, worth as much as the Mardi Gras beads for which women expose their breasts and tourists buy in gift shops year 'round. One theory is that this year's Mardi Gras is a Mardi Gras of locals. That everybody who was coming to New Orleans for the holiday was here by Saturday, and their presence--plus the drive-ins from nearby--made Saturday our big day, but that the local people, on their own, weren't enough to make a real Mardi Gras. Blame it on the aftermath of September 11th and (some) Americans still being afraid to travel.

Blame it on the moon, I think.

Another theory goes that it's the recession and the economic uncertainty people are feeling. According to that theory, the same number of people are here, they just aren't spending as much money as they did in the go-go Clinton years when everything was booming.

Pick your theory for why things don't work in a city where young people come to slack, and stay here drunk (or on junk), calling themselves the coolest of the cool, and old people with a work ethic are treated like a valuable commodity.

And you know what? Any theory will do.

Even a man stupid enough to try putting out fire with gasoline should be able to make it in this town during Mardi Gras--but I'm still waiting for you to prove it by me.

BRUSHSTROKES OF THE CITY

The ancient trees fight the concrete. Their ancient roots, lacing through the "new" New Orleans neighborhoods, create mini-cliffs, tearing up the slabs of stone, making even the sober stumble or watch their steps closely.

The vegetation of New Orleans is relentless. Even the trees. Their gnarled roots mock concrete and stone. They rip it up like falcon talons rip through the flesh of a rabbit. Strange vines grow over the sides of abandoned houses and reduce their walls to rubble, even devour entire yards, resisting the efforts of man to "tame" Nature. Gardeners tear the vines up by the roots, and every summer they manage to return.

In the older parts of the city, like the French Quarter or Marigny, where you live, there is the added (walking) hazard of sidewalks being paved with bricks rather than slabs of concrete like most cities. It is European in that way, like people say about San Francisco. The big difference is that New Orleans is not faux. Unlike San Francisco, the streets, and parts of the sewage and drainage system still extant, were built by the Spanish and French centuries ago. —

After you finish your first Mardi Gras on Bourbon Street, you are probably ready to party, especially after serving all those people partying. The difference is that they arrive fresh and you come to the party EXHAUSTED.

I am not just exhausted but hallucinatory. But The Rules of Sleep are nowhere in sight.

NEW ORLEANS - February, 2002

Everywhere I go, people have different advice (based on the lives they have chosen to live) on how I can stop being The Traveler. New Orleans is no different. When I told a co-worker I had never set foot in a Wal-Mart, she was nonplussed.

"Rod, you write the songs of cities. Cairo, Austin, San Franciso, London, Florence, New York, Baltimore, Hamilton, Belgrade, Virginia Beach, New Orleans. Your major failing is that you have not adopted any city as your own."

"You refuse to understand my affliction. I refuse to write about it."

"Your 'affliction'! What does that mean?"

"Some people understand that there is not only one affliction I'm afraid of... "

"Do you hate Wal-Marts?" she asked.

"No," I said. "I have no idea what they are like. They are not part of my experience. I have always lived in cities."

I am serving my last days at Casa de Caca, the half double shotgun I have shared with Matt and Caio since moving to New Orleans from Belgrade in July of 2001, God willing. I have told Matt I can't continue to tolerate the J.C. (Junkie Community of heroin addicts) and its vagaries--including the recurring practice of using this apartment as the public toilet for all their hangers-on. Matt says he doesn't want the problem, either, but he always opts for the lazy man's route, which means he doesn't have the courage to make any changes to his environment.

Just after I wrote this series of notes I learned that one of the more insidious J.C. members had recently gone to jail. This development should certainly change some of the lay of the land at Casa de Caca, but nowhere near enough to make me forget all that has gone before and in all probability will kick in again. The personnel of the J.C. might be changing, but I have lower hopes of its essential nature.

I've asked my boss, who's well-connected, and all of my friends, to keep their ears open for me. I've looked at a couple of apartments.

Now that I'm moonlighting as the janitor at O'Flaherty's bar in the French Quarter (this weekend I set up for Garrison Keillor's live broadcast from the pub), I can look forward to enough income to get my own place. I'm even open to sharing another place. Just not in this neighborhood. I don't want to be anywhere close to this heroin infestation if I can help it.

Thus, I find myself in a disengagement mode at Casa de Caca, investing less of myself there while exploring the other people and offerings of Nawlins. It feels good. The minor irritations--that no one will even do the simplest things like buy toilet paper, clean house, etc.--are endurable because I can see an end. In the process, I am meeting people who actually want to do something with their lives. I've committed to myself to know where I shall live next here in Nawlins by the end of the week.

Just the other night, among the new friends I am cultivating, I met an artist who did the "Yes! Oh yes!" response that I have come not to expect when I make reference to my Quest to find "Home." He immediately went into a jag of his own about how, for some people, there's always this sense of being a kind of emotional refugee, never feeling comfortable in a place--much as one might like it--because it just isn't "Home." He even went so far as to proclaim, rather excitedly, that the 'Net might be the only place for a community of people like "us" because there may not be a "civilized" country left to gather in or retreat to in geographic space. (I certainly hope he's wrong about that.)

But I am playing catch-up after the all-consuming time of Mardi Gras season, when service people like me are allowed little except (little) sleep outside of catering to the influx of merry-makers.

My friend Curtis, who is off to Belgium soon, reminds me that New Orleans is a Third World City, much better suited to somewhere in Central America. I have myself compared it to Haiti.

But I am also more and more aware that anyone's version of New

Orleans, even mine, says more about the interlocutor than about the Crescent City itself. Buyer beware.

NEW ORLEANS, 6 August, 2002

Everybody asks about Bourbon Street, the legendary theme park for adults, when they ask you about New Orleans. It's the center of the Mardi Gras celebrations for drunken revelers and people who believe they're getting a real taste of The Big Easy.

But among the cognoscenti of this storied town, the 21st Century hipsters, the place to be right now is a bit further down river. It's Frenchmen Street. Frenchmen Street has become so BIG and EASY in the last twelve months that the bridge crowd (people coming across the famed Causeway from the 'burbs), and tourists from France, Germany and the midwestern United States, think of it as their private treasure

They've figured out where the locals go for good live music seven nights a week and they're becoming addicted.

The jewel in the crown of Frenchmen Street, by many people's lights, is a club called The Spotted Cat.

New Orleans JazzFest is mentioned by print journals like Details as one of the must-do events for globetrotting party types. Two of the local bands that made the JazzFest cut, The Jazz Vipers and Hot Club, play every week at "The Cat" (as habitues call it) on Mondays and Thursdays respectively.

Trish Cone and her partner Ed Parrish had been in the bar business in New Orleans for years, but she had this dream of owning her own place that offered quality live music in an intimate setting. Kind of like sitting in your family parlor and having Miles Davis show up and jam. Nice dream.

She kept working and dreaming until she ran into David Berman, a friend, who suggested that she might want to look at a place on Frenchmen Street, in the Faubourg Marigny, hard on the French Quarter. It was a neighborhood that some folks back in the '90s felt had a lot of potential. Prices in the Quarter itself were going up. But Frenchmen Street was moribund. There were a couple of bars there, like the Tin Roof, that had gone through various incarnations, and the Apple Barrel and Snug Harbor. But these places were known more for the food in or near them, not music. The street was not even zoned for music.

But Trish wanted to own her own bar. She named it for her pet African cervil, Ninja -- a spotted cat.

The Spotted Cat opened at 623 Frenchmen Street in New Orleans in December, 2000. Then there was the problem of having live music. Talking with an assistant to Mayor Morial, Cone was told, "You want to do music? Do music. There's no such thing as Entertainment Police in New Orleans."

That proved to be good advice. When the Cat first started offering live music in April, 2001, only three of the eight clubs on Frenchmen offered live music, and that intermittently. Today, all the clubs on Frenchmen, anchored by the restaurants Belle Forché and the Marigny Brasserie, offer live music. The taxis come in and out of Frenchmen Street all night long with young, stylish people looking for the night life. During the afternoon, when the Cat offers "Happy Hour" prices from 2 until 6, southern gentleman reading Kipling and Wallace Stevens, local computer consultants, and the neighborhood crowd lounge and trade gibes with each other and the bartenders.

Besides the intimate music atmosphere (we'll talk about that below) the bartenders make the place and its ambience. All of the bartenders at The Spotted Cat are artists: three painters, a photographer, and a singer. The fact that they're not only bartenders raises the level of both the humor and the discourse at the place. Curtis, one of the bartenders, jokes that it's "a bar full of right-brain people". That's one of the charms of the Cat.

One rainy day, a group of jazz trumpeters who took refuge in the Cat decided to jam. They were playing for themselves. There were only three or four customers in the Cat. The jam became a musicians' party. Curtis, the bartender, calls this "A New Orleans Moment" and says that's why he loves this town. One of the patrons graced with that Moment commented, "This is what 52nd Street in Manhattan used to be all about."

Figure 3: The Royal Rounders at The Spotted Cat, where I bartended.

There are a lot of jaded bartenders in New Orleans. They have worked fourteen-hour shifts during Mardi Gras and learned to get an ATTITUDE toward visitors. The nice thing about the Cat is that, if you're a guest in The Big Easy, you don't get treated like dirt. You get treated just fine.

Music, with no cover charge, at the Cat started an infectious trend on Frenchmen Street. When I moved to New Orleans in July, 2001, it was still a little-known adjunct to the gutter-punk bars it connected to at the low end of Decatur Street. Today Checkpoint Charlie's and even the trendy Matador--where Vince Vaughn acts as Guest Bartender when he is in town--say they are at "Esplanade off Frenchmen". Last year they said "Esplanade and Decatur." You might get my drift.

BACK TO THE CAT: Last Monday, while the Jazz were playing at the Cat, Charmaine Neville and Kermit Ruffins came in and joined the set. Musicians love this place. It's like being at home. There's a sofa in front of the bandstand where patrons sit with their friends lounging in "safari" wicker chairs. The bartenders bring in their favorite CDs to fill the time during the bands' breaks.

The Secret of Success for the Cat is the music. Well, the musicians and the magic they make in this little room. It's almost impossible to walk past The Spotted Cat when the music is playing. Visitors to New Orleans, after seeing Bourbon Street, who start to actually explore New Orleans, find themselves on Frenchmen at the Cat on a lazy afternoon, fleeing the sweltering heat, and say, "I wish I'd known about this place when I got here." Now they do. So do you, but don't ruin it for the rest of us if you come here. Keep it the intimate, cordial space you found when you arrived. Thank you.

Things go slow in New Orleans. What do you do when the Heat Index tells you that it feels like 110 degrees Fahrenheit, even if the thermometer says it's only 96?

You mosey, I suspect. You amble and take things a little easy. Except here in New Orleans folks take things a Big Easy. That means things don't quite happen when they were planned. You spend your time in a saloon with nice air conditioning, and the next thing you know the music is more intoxicating than the booze and you find yourself talking to someone you never met before about things that matter. Lots of things. It's easy.

The Spotted Cat is a reincarnated bar from the earlier years, fifty years ago, when the fisherman on the Mississippi River would come back into town. That long-ago bar was supplanted by an oyster processing plant and, briefly, a dress shop. Frenchmen Street, as recently as six years ago, was a place to avoid, as was much of the Marigny. There were whores and drug dealers and crime as bad as East Baltimore.

By the '90s, New Orleans was ready to clean itself up. That process is still going on. Frenchmen Street is an example of what can happen when you get it right and reclaim your town. Trish and Ed were lucky enough to come here at the right time.

There are jokes going around you in a place like Nawlins. A lot of them have to do with the endless summer and the hot-hot-hot nature of things. How many liters of sweat; how hot it is in the shade; when you have 4-6 months of summer, the weather man should not be talking about how soon it will be summer again, as my pal Matt says.

It's analogous to living with a sun shining down on you at midnight or a full moon that never, ever goes away.

That's why this subterranean, above-ground-crypts feel of New Orleans makes everything about the life a dreamy thing. That might explain all the ghost stories, the way you imagine waifs moving just along your peripheral vision. There. Not there. That's why a place like The Spotted Cat can be like a long, sweet draught of lemonade when you most need it.

SPOTTED CAT DRAMATIS PERSONNAE

   * JAK has been around since the beginning. He left for a while, but now he's back. Grizzled and wiry, the guy has more off-beat charm than any single mortal deserves. I'm still trying to figure out why he wants to call me "Don."
   * JULIE is another long-timer at this venue. She's a handsome blonde with a kind of mature, cosmopolitan grace that makes her easy to be around.
   * DANIEL is tall and jovial with a smile that reminds you of a playground friend. He moves fast and talks almost so. You can imagine him as a forward guard.
   * LINNZI is the new kid on the block. She sings with the Jazz Vipers and oozes wholesome. Picture Pipi Longstocking with blonde hair. Is it right that this woman should be dealing with drunks?
   * CURTIS and Mayor Ray Nagin were separated at birth. I have this on the authority of their personal barber. We all know that we should enjoy His Awesomeness's company as long as we can. One day he and his wife will build that house in Belize and we'll never see him again.

The Nouvelle New Orleans that is being offered to a new generation of visitors is still bohemian; this town couldn't stop being Boho if it wanted to, and it's still The South, for better or worse.

What's different about the vibe (pardon my hippie-speak) is that it's not like a frat party or a theme park, it's authentic in the unadulterated way you'd expect at St. Nick's in Harlem or San Francisco's old Mabuhay Gardens. You don't get those types of moments enough in this life.

LISTEN: The Wurlitzer piano at the Cat was built in 1953. Its serial number is 459161. Until it was bought by Trish Cone and her partner Ed in 1992, it had never moved far from Bourbon Street and it had been played by a series of great New Orleans jazz pianists.

Like our Second Lines down here, those celebratory jazz funeral marches that had a wonderful representation in the Lana Turner film, "Imitation of Life", the artifacts of life are carried to the Afterworld on a river of music.

The original owner of this Wurlitzer piano at The Spotted Cat was Steve Pistorius. He primed the instrument for a series of jazz players over the next fifty years. John Royan, Steve and Lars Edegran, Topsy Chapman, Marva Wright, Thais Clark, James Booker, Chris Burke, Barry Martyn, Ron Simpson, and Wendall Eugene. Trumpeter Doc Cheatham brought his piano man to a party for Trish and Ed to play it. Jeff Hamilton, Bob Brockman, et alia, played the same lovely ivories in succession,

"Mr. Bob" Brockman played that piano only a week ago, another quiet Sunday afternoon spiced with the soothing chime that only a piano's percussive and fluid flow can create.

When the piano was moved from Toulouse to Frenchmen Street, pianist David Roe ("DR" of the band The Royal Rounders and a bartender at Coop's Place on Decatur Street), played rollicking riffs on the back of the moving truck all the way through the French Quarter. He hit his crescendo on the doorstep of The Spotted Cat.

THE MUSIC

The Jazz Vipers are the kind of band that makes the likes of Harry Dean Stanton feel comfortable getting up and doing a song for the assembled guests at The Spotted Cat. They are serious and professional and just fun to hear. They were booked for this year's

JazzFest but had to bow out and let their pals Hot Club fill the slot because of other commitments.

Nobody comes away from hearing the Vipers without a smile. They are part of what makes the Cat happen for locals and visitors alike. You have to be a hot draw to make people come out on a Monday night.

I guess it was about a week after the preceding article was published that my pal, Scott Salin, told me that Trish Cone was looking for me.

Trish Cone is a lovely redhead whose resplendent smile belies her age. She's about my age, but you couldn't prove it by looking at her. She owned The Spotted Cat with her partner, Ed Parrish.

I thought, Oh-oh! Did I get one of my facts wrong? If you're a journalist, that's your biggest nightmare. But I was sure I hadn't. I was in the mood for a cocktail that Saturday afternoon. I went down to The Cat with Scott and ordered a Scotch.

Trish came in shortly after we arrived. She came up and hugged me with tears in her eyes. "You love this place as much as I do, don't you?" she said. I nodded, relieved.

"I read what you wrote about us," she said. "It was wonderful. Thank you."

She turned to Curtis, who was bartending at the time, and asked, "You can train him on our system tomorrow, right?" Curtis looked at me and said, "Whenever you're ready, man."

I took another sip of my Scotch. It sounded like I had just been hired as the new bartender at The Cat. "Tomorrow's good," I said. I had become one of the dramatis personnae of The Cat.

The New Orleans Way.

I fear that that kind of moment, that kind of New Orleans Moment --
where a right-brain person like myself, a writer who had once been a
bartender, would get hired as a bartender simply by dint of writing a
paean to a place he loved and treasured will get a job because he wrote
about his love--will not happen in the "new" New Orleans that people
are talking about building now.

Chapter 3

LIZARD LICK, NC - 2 September, 2005

New Orleans Mayor C. Ray Nagin released a plea to the world with the headline "S.O.S. A Night of Hell." A hotel in downtown New Orleans is on fire, he said. There was a chemical explosion at four a.m. that was burning out of control, too. So those people now stranded in front of the Ernest Morial Convention Center have grown even more desperate and violent. While some of them were having a shoot-out with the police, at least one woman had a baby without medical care.

It is a tradition in New Orleans that candidates for political office become Guest Bartenders at Molly's at the Market, a local pub on Decatur Street that was the locus of the lives of many of us in the French Quarter. So C. Ray Nagin did his time behind the bar to garner our votes. That's where I first met him.

Speaking as a person who had to do mixology to pay his rent, I have to say that Ray did a passable job. He not only made a decent cocktail, but he didn't look nervous dealing with the people of his city. He was jovial, polite, sometimes funny. He was the kind of person that even the most jaded of us in New Orleans could imagine talking with over a beer at the end our work day. A stand-up guy.

Whether you asked him about civic responsibility or the last Saints game, he had something to say you could appreciate.

Now Ray is the Mayor of New Orleans, the city we have lost, and he has stepped up to challenge the bureaucrats in Louisiana and Washington, particularly challenging the Office of Homeland Security, to ask why so many of the people we loved are now likely dead.

After Ray's election, I asked one of the writers for my online magazine to interview him. He had intelligent answers about trying to manage one of the toughest cities to manage in America. But he was focusing on trying to build a technological infrastructure to augment the only industry our city had left, tourism. Ray wasn't thinking about The Big One, the hurricane that would create a disaster in America of biblical proportions. Nobody was.

NEW ORLEANS, Esplanade Avenue – 2 October, 2002

I must remind myself that every silver lining that would venture my way comes with its requisite cloud attached. I might as well be living under a bridge when I have a profligate flatmate who takes in stray miscreants, without consultation, the way old Italian ladies adopt stray cats. "Oh. I see: while you were drunk (again) you ran into a crackhead and decided that it was a good idea that he move in with us. Thank you very much.

"What's that? The crackhead is definitely moving out tomorrow? Okay. Is that like he was definitely moving out yesterday?"

Then I receive a telephone call informing me that "we" are moving uptown, a couple of blocks away from the Bon Temps Roulez, a popular bar in that area. We certainly don't need to move close to another bar, I was thinking. Wait a minute, I'm working on at The Spotted Cat on Tuesday! It's the day I take deliveries from the vendors and stock the bar. I can't move, too. Did anybody ask me? What's this place look like? And the crackhead is moving in with us there, too?

"What do you mean 'we', Kemo Sabe?"

On Monday evening I sat down with with my roommate Brian in the courtyard of our building, one of the oldest on Esplanade, to explain to him why I was disinclined to move anywhere with him and the new refugee.

  * I was awakened in the wee hours of Friday evening by the two roisterers and a blaring conclusion to the movie "How the West Was Won" coming from the suddenly enlivened television set. There was noise and confusion all around me. Something about the other guy exchanging clothes with a woman in a bar bathroom.

They made frantic calls for take-out food. The other guy scaled the walls around our courtyard at some point and cracked open his head. Brian locked him out of the apartment and passed out. There was loud calling and banging on our door for about fifteen minutes or so until Brian woke up. More chatter.

* On Saturday, they didn't work for some reason. Brian came to The Spotted Cat, where I was bartending and got faced. After a few hours he was buying drinks for people he'd never met . He was ordering drinks and knocking them over on the bar after that. I had to kick his ass out.

* On Sunday, the sousing continued and things were starting to look bad.

* On Monday, he had borrowed money from both Scott and myself. The money he got from me was supposed to be for transportation to work. I never asked what he had told Scott. I was already at my wit's end, but had to spend one more evening with Darryl before he flew out of town. I was not about to move uptown into what would inevitably be continuing chaos, far away from the one stable circumstance in my life, the bartending job.

Tuesday there was a flurry of phone calls. I'm sure I exceeded my quota on the cell phone. There were charges and counter-charges among my coterie of friends. Nobody was being quite straight with anybody else, in order to preserve civility.

I worked my shift at the bar, performing the jovial and light-hearted role patrons expect from a good bartender, while Hurricane Lili continued on her direct path for New Orleans.

It was going to be a real hurricane this time, all of my friends warned me. It was going to be bad, they predicted.

Brian and the crackhead were having a falling out. I received a call telling me not to go back to the apartment at the end of my shift at the bar. There was something about calling the police. I decided I would sort all that out later.

My friend Darryl had been in town over the weekend, so when not working my shifts at the Cat, I had been out and about with him. I saw the gathering clouds on the horizon, or at least sensed them, but I was trying to keep the best face on things so dear Darryl would not worry for me.

By the time Darryl flew out of New Orleans on Tuesday morning and I checked back into the world, the twin storms of Brian (with whom I've been staying) and Lili (who'd become a Category Two hurricane) were both moving to change my life.

Scott was going back and forth with our friend Mary McGinn, the realtor, about getting me out of that place on Esplandade Avenue and as far away from Brian as possible post haste. There was subterfuge and intrigue in the air. We would rendezvous at a car down the street taking separate paths. My laptop and I were whisked away into the night. I was upset that I didn't even have a toothbrush. Now my clothes and my zip drive and toiletries were in one location, my remaining CDs, other clothes and books were still at Shawn's, my laptop and I are at a third location. What little I have of a life is now scattered all over the French Quarter. And Lili is scheduled to make landfall here tomorrow afternoon.

All this in the life of a man who insists he doesn't want or need any drama in his life. I have been sucked into the vortex that is The Black Hole of New Orleans.

People are battening down the hatches and boarding up their storefronts again. Cars are being moved to secure parking garages or at to least higher ground. "You'll have something to write about his time!" Scott quips.

What obtains today can only be called gallows humor. We look at the various representations of Hurricane Lili rushing toward us, with those ratings-winning Weather Channel graphics, and joke about the worst.

Most of the people here in the French Quarter make dates to meet their friends at the closest open bar and have a hurricane party. "We are all in this together." The popular sentiment seems to be that since most of us here on the high ground (the Quarter is the highest point in this city, which is why it all started here) won't suffer as much as people on the Lake (Pontchartrain) front or on the coastal islands, so why not use it as another excuse to get drunk or to drown?

"What were you doing when New Orleans was washed into the sea, Daddy?"

"Well, Darlin', as I recall, I was eating a salami sandwich and waiting for my inflatable bed to fill up. I figured I could float out of town on that, or wait for the helicopters to spot me bobbing along. Which is about what happened, as your mother could tell you.

"They found me five hours after Lili had passed over, clutching my laptop to my chest and just riding the whitecaps like God's own surfer. I had told my friends days before that I was a survivor and I was pleased to be proved right once again.

"Your mother was one of the Coast Guard personnel on that there chopper that day and you were just a twinkle in my eye ... "

Both these storms were coming at me from behind, I felt. Like Tupac, I was staring at the world of hurt coming toward me through my rearview mirror, while smiling to my friend Darryl and telling him everything is all right. Don't worry. I'm a survivor.

The running joke here in New Orleans is that when The Big One hits, the Army Corps of Engineers will just roll out the 50,000 body bags they've been keeping in storage for such an eventuality and come gather our bodies when the water finally recedes. The sun breaks through the clouds now and again, but the wind is picking up.

(If all of the foregoing seems a bit muddled, I'm not surprised. I'm a bit muddled myself right now.)

I'm in a strange--if spacious and quiet--apartment, taking refuge from the drama. "You need a little down time," the friend who's lent me his apartment advises.

I conceded to this rescue operation reluctantly. I have quiet, but nothing else, not even my clothes. I would like to retrieve them before Lili arrives.

As I mentioned to Darryl on his last evening in town, everything in my life seems to turn on a dime. I have A Plan, of sorts, once I retrieve the few belongings I brought to New Orleans with me from Europe: I have both the Realtors I know best here looking for a "writer's garret". One is e-mailing all the listings she can gather for me today. The other is talking with clients who are also friends. Even if I have only the job at the bar, I should be able to manage something small. I now realize the roommate thing, despite its economic advantages, is against my nature. At my age, having control of my environment is all-important. I'm flexible, but too much spontaneity is as bad as none at all.

My time house-sitting for Scott reminded me of my old life, of the pleasures of being able to retreat from the noise of the world. I treasure silence--especially in this country, which seems obsessed with closing out ones own thoughts with the ceaseless chatter of CNN headlines, the cacophony of radio, the hyena giggle of laugh tracks, the blaring of jukeboxes, the roar of the madding crowd. SHUT UP!

I long to cook a meal myself, again, as well. I enjoy cooking. But since my couch-surfing days began last summer, I have been on a steady diet of takeout and delivery food. That is no way to live. It never costs less than doing things oneself. That is one of the prices of being a nomad.

3 OCTOBER, 2002

Hurricane Lili arrived at approximately 3 a.m. this morning to entertain us.

She did not hit New Orleans dead-on. But the news of her imminent arrival was enough for them to close the levee floodgates at 3:00 p.m. yesterday and send my poor friend Jamie Menutis, who lives on Lake Pontchartrain, packing again for the second week in a row. I spoke with the frustrated young woman last night. This time Interstate 10, the escape route for those wanting to evacuate our fishbowl, became a big parking lot by yesterday afternoon. Meanwhile, she tells me, the governor of Mississippi--whose state has had a long-standing agreement with the state of Louisiana to open four lanes of traffic for exiting denizens--has declared "No way" on honoring the agreement this time, and has left only two lanes for Louisianians to flee into his state. Tough noogies.

The arrival of my second storm of the week awakened me from a foreboding nightmare. I am deep in the French Quarter now. I closed all the shutters before continuing to edit articles for my Web magazine..

At three a.m. I was awakened by the rattling shutters and the sound of pouring rain. Because of the closed shutters, I could only peer out at the darkness through the cracks. It was raining hard, but not horrific. There was wind but not a gale. This morning it is barely raining at all. I might go for a walk around nine to see if there's actually anything to be afraid about.

My predictions never work out. It's nearly eleven and I'm still trying to finish my editing. It rained sporadically this morning, but as I type this, there's only more wind. So I plan to walk across the Quarter to eat lunch as soon as I finish this entry.

Scott calls to say that he's going to pick up his car, which he'd stored in a parking garage, as we'd "dodged the bullet" again. I'll act like I'm surprised, considering what I saw of Lili last night and this morning. Those folks at the Weather Channel must certainly be proud of themselves--or laughing about the gullibility of people in southern Louisiana. It's a nifty trick to pull the same fearmongering two weeks in a row. Even Orson Welles didn't have the 'nads to try that.

And once again just about everything in New Orleans is boarded up and shut down... except the bars.

LIZARD LICK, North Carolina - 8 September, 2005

No, it wasn't like we weren't expecting a hurricane one day to wash us away and out of New Orleans. We knew what we were in for, just like people living in California know that one day it won't be only a shaking bed in the night; it will actually be The Big One and their asses will be gone.

It just happened for New Orleans first.

We had always known in New Orleans about those body bags they had waiting for us. With the fatalism characteristic of romantics and drunks, we joked about those body bags and how one day--who knew when--rather than waking up from the latest storm off the Gulf of Mexico, we would be zipped up and carted away. Let's face it, almost thirty percent of the people in town didn't even own a damned car. Most of that thirty percent were black people but they--we--were not the only ones.

We all believed that, because of our natural bonhomie, people would take care of each other. That is part of the New Orleans Way.

But we didn't factor in the crackheads, heroin addicts and ex-convicts who were also part of our daily lives and lived cheek-by-jowl with us in our neighborhoods. Like most people in America, we looked the other way and never anticipated disaster as it really plays out. Why should we? Life was not good but it was as good as it could get in the American Haiti. If you were smart or had some connections, one day, maybe--well, surely--you would get out. You could always come back to New Orleans to party with your friends, but everybody knew that staying in New Orleans, unless you had the anchor of family, was just damned nuts.

That city that we all said we loved could kill you if you were not careful. It was the murder capital of America for too many years running. New Orleans and Baltimore used to fight over who could kill the most people in a single year. Baltimore managed to have less than three hundred killed in a single year. That put New Orleans on top.

If you lived in New Orleans, you knew that between the drugs and the booze and the just plain ignorance of too many folks, in a place where just about every house had at least one gat (gun, weapon), and all of life was fueled by a volatile mix of sultry tropical weather, passion, and lunacy, somebody was bound to get shot today.

That too is the New Orleans Way.

Over three hundred people were killed every year in New Orleans for as long as anyone can remember.

In the Sunday (4 September 2005), edition of the New York Daily News, Errol Louis had this to write ("Why We Couldn't Save the People of New Orleans"):

By almost every statistical measure, New Orleans is a bad place to be poor. Half the city's households make less than $28,000 a year, and 28% of the population lives in poverty.

In the late 1990s, the state's school systems ranked dead last in the nation in the number of computers per student (1 per 88), and Louisiana has the nation's second-highest percentage of adults who never finished high school. By the state's own measure, 47% of the public schools in New Orleans rank as "academically unacceptable."

And Louisiana is the only one of the 50 states where the state legislature doesn't allocate money to pay for the legal defense of indigent defendants. The Associated Press reported this year that it's not unusual for poor people charged with crimes to stay in jail for nine months before getting a lawyer appointed.

In his article Mr. Louis went on to talk about circumstances and conditions that we in New Orleans certainly knew about as the features of our everyday lives, from scandalously corrupt politicians––he quotes former congressman Billy Tauzin's statement that "… half of Louisiana is under water and the other half is under indictment"––to an even more notoriously corrupt political infrastructure. He expresses outrage at situations we in Nawlins would joke about. Like the fact that, adjusted for Louisiana's population size, our state had more elected officials convicted of crimes than any of the other 49. Or that in recent years Louisiana had fourteen state judges convicted of assorted crimes.

There were at least fifty (50) officers of the New Orleans Police Department (NOPD) convicted of murder, rape, robbery and extortion in just the last ten years. And when Katrina hit, two former members of the NOPD were on Death Row.

We always assumed that the rest of the country knew about all this. You could read about what was going on down there in the local paper, the Times-Picayune, and sometimes even in places like the Washington Post. So now with everybody wringing their hands about the "discovery" of how bad things were for folks down in New Orleans--well, I for one, just have to wonder.

Chapter 4

ANGER

Anne Rice is angry. Ray Nagin is angry. And I am angry, too.
America failed its people.

So, I wrote this on the Wednesday, three days into the tragedy, after
Katrina took my city, my brutal lover, New Orleans away:

LIZARD LICK, North Carolina - 31 August, 2005

THE FACTS ARE GRIM AND COLD: Nearly a million people who
once lived in the greater New Orleans metropolitan area are now
refugees in their own country.

In the aftermath of the Hurricane Katrina disaster, one of the worst
natural disasters in the history of the United States, in a just world,
there would be an investigation into how this catastrophe could have
been avoided. We suspect, as this report will explain, that much of the
blame should be put squarely at the doorstep of the Bush
administration in the United States.

It is not at all difficult to assert that New Orleans has died for Iraq.
Money that could have shored up that city's infrastructure, money
requested by the Army Corps of Engineers for just that purpose, was
instead allocated to pay off contracts for the reconstruction of the
newly-occupied Middle East nation and line the pockets of executives
at Halliburton subsidiary Kellogg, Brown & Root.

But first, the story as it is unfolding today on the ground.

It has only been two days since Louisiana governor Kathleen Blanco
entered the Superdome in New Orleans to assess the condition of the
refugees from Hurricane Katrina. When she came out of the damaged
and leaking building, dazed, all she could say was that conditions
inside the structure were "very, very desperate."

Calling friends out of state on their cell phones, refugee families reported that food and water had already run out, toilets were backing up, the air conditioners had failed, and people were turning violent. One man, distraught, had apparently committed suicide. At least one young girl was said to have been sexually assaulted during the night. Conditions were grim, to say the least.

As this is written, on Wednesday, 31 August 2005, the refugees who had huddled in the Superdome in downtown New Orleans during the ravages of Katrina, and people from other parts of the city who have been helicoptered or boated by the Coast Guard from their rooftops, are being evacuated to Houston, Texas, where they are to be temporarily sheltered in another sports stadium, the Astrodome.

The Fox News television channel has reveled in showing pictures of black looters in New Orleans over the past forty-eight hours. CNN interviews a man who escaped the raging waters of the flooding city by hanging on, for dear life, to a piece of wood, even as he watched his own wife drown in the deluge. He said he wishes now that he had died, too, because he has lost everything and cannot go on.

Officials agree that nearly nothing was done on Tuesday to staunch the flood wall through which flood waters have consumed eighty percent (80%) of the Crescent City. All available vehicles and aircraft were being used to save people instead. The bodies of the dead are being pushed aside in order to get to those still living. The body count will come later, when infrastructure is repaired, the streets are pumped dry and all the remaining refugees are recovered and evacuated.

Coffins from the above-ground graves of earlier generations of New Orleanians can be seen floating from helicopters passing above, still looking for live victims.

Katrina did not seem like The Big One on Monday, when she jogged right, toward the east, and failed to hit New Orleans dead on. But the levees had never been tested by a storm this forceful. The Army Corps of Engineers said the levees were built to withstand a Category Three hurricane, but a Category Three had not struck New Orleans since the new levees were constructed, so everyone knew that forecast was speculative rather than proven.

All of us who lived in New Orleans used to joke about the 10,000--or was it 25,000 or 50,000--body bags Orleans Parish had stored up to deposit us in when The Big One, the killer hurricane that was inevitable, finally slammed into town from up the mouth of the Mississippi River. But nobody was quick to move away.

Life was good in New Orleans. Some bar, somewhere nearby, was always open, 24 and 7, there were tourists enough to fleece (except in the summer), and plenty of good food all around. The Big Easy. Bon temps roulez. A predominantly black, dirt-poor city with no industry to speak of, no significant change in one hundred years, and the biggest booze, drugs, gambling and sex problems on the North American continent. A hell hole and a drunkard's dream if you ever did see one.

Katrina hit at the end of the summer, a time when most of the population of New Orleans, who are predominantly service industry workers, are dead broke or just scraping along waiting for the sweltering heat to go away and the tourists to come back. On Tuesday, the day after the storm had passed, the flooding began. It was over 90 degrees Fahrenheit in New Orleans and there was no potable water.

The electricity was down and it was impossible for people to call into telephone area code 504 all day. At one point during the day, Tuesday, there was only guesswork as to what was going on in the Big Easy because all normal forms of communication were down.

Could a disaster of these proportions, with nearly a million people stranded, have been averted? Perhaps. Part of the problem, what Governor Blanco now calls trying to fill a "black hole," repairing the five hundred foot hole in the flood wall at the 17th Street Canal, might have been averted. The latest solution floated by the Army Corps of Engineers is to plug the hole by inserting a barge. But this failure to adequately prepare the levee and flood wall system of New Orleans goes back a few months to a rejected budget request to the Bush administration.

NEW ORLEANS DIES FOR IRAQ

In an article in Editor and Publisher on Tuesday, 30 August, 2005
("Did New Orleans Catastrophe Have to Happen? 'Times-Picayune'
Had Repeatedly Raised Federal Spending Issues") by Will Bunch, this
passage stands out:

When flooding from a massive rainstorm in May 1995 killed six
people, Congress authorized the Southeast Louisiana Urban Flood
Control Project, or SELA.

Over the next 10 years, the Army Corps of Engineers, tasked with
carrying out SELA, spent $430 million on shoring up levees and
building pumping stations, with $50 million in local aid. But at
least $250 million in crucial projects remained, even as hurricane
activity in the Atlantic Basin increased dramatically and the levees
surrounding New Orleans continued to subside.

Yet after 2003, the flow of federal dollars toward SELA dropped to a
trickle. The Corps never tried to hide the fact that the spending
pressures of the war in Iraq, as well as homeland security--coming
at the same time as federal tax cuts--was the reason for the
strain. At least nine articles in the Times-Picayune from 2004 and
2005 specifically cite the cost of Iraq as a reason for the lack of
hurricane- and flood-control dollars.

Newhouse News Service, in an article posted late Tuesday night at The
Times-Picayune web site, reported: "No one can say they didn't see it
coming... Now in the wake of one of the worst storms ever, serious
questions are being asked about the lack of preparation."

In early 2004, as the cost of the conflict in Iraq soared, President
Bush proposed spending less than 20 percent of what the Corps said
was needed for Lake Pontchartrain, according to a Feb. 16, 2004,
article, in New Orleans CityBusiness.

On June 8, 2004, Walter Maestri, emergency management chief for
Jefferson Parish, Louisiana; told the Times-Picayune: "It appears that
the money has been moved in the president's budget to handle

homeland security and the war in Iraq, and I suppose that's the price we pay. Nobody locally is happy that the levees can't be finished, and we are doing everything we can to make the case that this is a security issue for us."

In other words, it was the policy of the United States government to leave New Orleans to twist slowly in the wind, even after the horrific hurricane season of 2004.

Oh wait, the implication would be that accepting that hurricanes are becoming more severe because the oceans' waters are getting warmer, particularly in the Gulf Stream, would be an admission that scientists are correct and there should be concern about global warming.

Not on Mr. Bush's watch.

WE HAVE NOWHERE TO GO

One million former New Orleanians find themselves at the mercy of the kindness of strangers in other cities. The governor of Louisiana and the mayor of New Orleans have told them not to come back home. So other cities and other people have to take them in until the water is pumped out of the soup bowl, the toxic sludge is cleaned up, and the bodies are all taken away.

I had written in my diaristic journal:

30 August 2005- 10:49 p.m. EDT: Well, we all know by now that if I still lived in New Orleans, particularly down in the lower 9th Ward (to which I was relegated after being kicked out of the place I was living in the Treme), I would be one of those people standing on a rooftop waiting to be discovered.

But I'm not in New Orleans. Once again The Great Mystery helped me dodge a bullet.

There are a lot of my friends from Nawlins I'd like to try to contact right now: Scott and Tierney, Greg and Teresa, JW and Elizabeth,

Mary, Dave and Jenno, Leszek and Carolina, my girl Tanya... I have the comfort of knowing Matt is sitting warm and toasty somewhere in Florida, probably watching The Weather Channel or "Larry King Live" on CNN to see if there's a shot of his house or the street where his job used to be. He's likely clutching a cocktail and thinking, "Got out just in time."

Nick's house, where I lived before my last month in Nawlins, before shacking with Shawn for a month and moving to North Carolina, is probably heavily damaged, since it bordered the Industrial Canal. I heard the Governor of Louisiana, Ms. Blanco, say tonight to Larry King that there is no potable water in Orleans Parish right now and that St. Bernard Parish is demolished. It's almost out of that Randy Newman song entitled, "Louisiana 1927." He sang,

They gonnah wash us away, wash us away ...

No lie.

After being frustrated trying to reach friends from New Orleans about whom I was concerned, the Internet became the next option. Most of my friends are smart enough to have evacuated the city when the warnings came. Many of them likely would be somewhere with Internet access. It was worth a shot.

It was hard not remembering the good times, the bad times, and all the faces of people had I seen on both sides of the bar during the years I lived in Nawlins. I started thinking back to what I first believed would be the opening passage of this book:

NEW ORLEANS, Esplanade Avenue, 19 April, 2005

Flashman has lived in New Orleans for seven years now. He is my friend. We lived in the same apartment twice. He has lived there all along. He never moves; he is like a stone. He has been at the same job for four years, though he hates the job. Drink, work; drink, work; that is the definition of Flashman's life. He is a big man with a big heart, but not a great deal of education or ambition.

Figure 4: Holiday decorations on a house on Esplanade Avenue.

Flashman is one of those invisible, nearly faceless, service workers that keep the tourism industry in New Orleans going. But he is not faceless when he gets off work, has a bit of money in his pocket and drinks whiskey after his beers. Then he becomes a Holy Terror.

The next morning--or evening, if he arrives at his apartment at daybreak or eight a.m.--he doesn't remember a bit of what Holy Terror did to you the night before. Not a syllable or a blow, as the case may be. He doesn't remember the dark power of his rage.

"You remember that money you gave me for rent two days ago?"

"I remember everything. That is my curse."

"Gone. All gone. It went straight to my liver."

"You said you were having a good time."

"A good time most of which I can't even remember."

"You remember talking to me when you got home yesterday morning?"

"I did?"

"I had to let you in. You couldn't find the hole, Shaquile."

"Asshole."

"Glad you remember my nickname."

"What time did I get back?"

"I don't know. About 8:30 I guess."

"So I was out from two until 8:30 in the morning? No wonder I feel like hammered shit today."

"You left at 12:30."

"No way!"

"You came back from your job, took a nap, and got up at about midnight, showered and left. Before your nap you said you were meeting your bartender friend at two. I was surprised you got up so early."

"12:30?"

"12:30."

"Dude, the last thing I remember is making out in the bar with this fifty-five year old woman who says her name is Peanut-Butter-and-Jelly."

"Going for older women now?"

"It's not the first time I've met her down there." He paused and got this strange look on his face. "There's something about her that fascinates me."

"So you're sucking face with a woman in her fifties in public, in a bar. The train had already left the station, I gather."

"Yeah. No chance I'd be able to hit chicks my age after that."

"Ya think?"

"I just straight-up blacked out."

"Okay. Not the first time, after all. If I were you, I'd write it off to 'youthful enthusiasm.'"

"I don't know why I do this to myself."

"Take my advice and eat something, Bubula. You'll feel better."

"Think so?"

"Never argue with your bartender."

"Last week you were claiming you weren't a bartender anymore, Dude!"

"Once a bartender... "

"We got beerage?"

"We managed to go to the store last night while you were out carousing, if that's what you're asking. We realized that someone might get home shit-faced and ask for a brew."

"Dickhead."

"There you go again. Let's restrict it to one epithet. I'm getting used to 'Asshole.'"

"Asshole."

"I knew you were a quick study."

LIZARD LICK, North Carolina - 31 August, 2005

I was going to start the book that way because that is a scene that everyone in New Orleans can easily relate to. New Orleans is the only place I've ever known where people could call in late for work because they had a hangover from the night before and openly admit it, especially during Mardi Gras.

Hell, you were lucky in New Orleans if your boss didn't call you to say he or she would be late because they were still half in the bag from a wild night in the French Quarter. So watching the worst on CNN and The Weather Channel it suddenly struck me that I was going into a state of mourning.

As much as my relationship with New Orleans had always been love/hate, I had to admit that I was losing someone/something/some special place in my heart that I had loved. I had never doubted until Tuesday afternoon that I would return to New Orleans whenever I got the chance.

Now, I knew, sadly, tragically, with a lump in my throat, that the New Orleans in my memory--the New Orleans I had written about and breathed in like the jasmine-scented air on Esplanade Avenue--that New Orleans would never exist again.

The e-mails I got from the few friends I could reach confirmed this fact. They were shell-shocked.

Matt wrote to me from Tallahassee, Florida:

It seemed like everything would be OK earlier yesterday, and then we went out for a few drinks, came home and saw on the news that the levee had broken and "80% of the city is underwater". While I am on somewhat sorta kinda high ground, I *did* see some footage shot off of I-10 of the Circle Food Store on Claiborne & St. Bernard Ave...and it looked like there was 8-10 feet of water in there. Not a good sign. But that *is* a bit away from my place. Maybe, just maybe, I'm on high enough ground that there's little or no water in the house. I can only hope. I have my most important stuff with me, but still, the concept of losing my stereo, almost all my CDs, that huge DVD collection I've been burning over the last year, my entire literature collection, my old photos, blah blah blah, everything except the computer, the guitar, and a duffel bag full of clothes...it's hard to really comprehend it.

I have to assume that I no longer have a job, since it may take months to get that water out of there (plus time to clean up the toxic sludge), it seems to me that it will be impossible to SELL uninhabitable real estate. So my services will most likely not be needed.

I have $200 in cash and $300 in the bank, and that's it. Next destination is Kentucky, and after I get there I will begin deliberating on a course of action. Probably my best bet would be to go back to San Diego and survey the scene from there. Maybe head back to SF and kick it with Mark or Pen Girl.

Later in day I heard from Jamie Menutis, who used to write for my magazine. She lived on the lake front. I remember calling her during the night of Hurricane Isidore hitting New Orleans, years earlier, to make certain she was all right. On Tuesday, she wrote in her e-mail:

we are safe, though i fear we have lost everything that we own.

i am in new york now and trying to make my way to houston. my daughter managed to save her dogs-i am happy about this. Having worked with refugees, i now understand that nothing material matters except your life in the end. we will be fine, because we are alive.

Later I heard from Greg Cowman, an inveterate jokester, a fellow bartender who worked at the Napoleon House on St. Louis and Chartres before Katrina and had once worked with me at the Spotted Cat on Frenchmen Street in the Marigny. I had trained Greg at that bar, in fact. We had become great friends. He had taken me to the airport when I left New Orleans for an abortive stay in Phoenix in 2004. He had been one of my mainstays when I returned to New Orleans in early 2005. Greg wrote in his e-mail:

Hey Rod -

Just a short note to let you know that Teresa, her youngest daughter, and I are safe and out of harms way. We drove up to Teresa's oldest daughter's place in Baton Rouge on Saturday. We all have beds, food, water, electricity, and basically everything we need. We are VERY LUCKY.

I don't know anything about my apartment or its contents, but I do have enough renters insurance to cover any loses. Actually, unless the big pecan tree fell onto the house or the roof got torn off, I doubt there will be any major damage to my stuff. But, then again, I don't have any idea what the place looks like. I just hope my landlord, her 96 year old mother, and my neighbor had the sense and wherewithal to get out of town in time.

Teresa's house, on the other hand, is probably gone. Slidell was pretty much ground zero and the water level is still rising as I type.

She, of course, has insurance. Whether she will have a job may be another story, but will deal with that when necessary. Obviously, I can get a bartending job anywhere, if/when push comes to shove. Ironically, I had just gotten a low interest loan a few days before the storm hit, so I have enough cash flow for a while. I suppose the Napoleon House will be back in business someday, but not for at least a couple of months. Then again, maybe not ...

So, life in New Orleans will never ever be the same. We don't have a clue as to our next step, but I'm sure we will make a new beginning somewhere.

We are truly thankful to be alive.

I can't help wondering how many people I (we) know may not be with us today. It boggles the mind.

I am glad that you weren't here to suffer through this nightmare.

I hope you are well.

Write when you have a minute, but I realize you have LOTS of friends here who may not have been as fortunate as I, who need your attention more.

There's so much more to say, but we are all pretty drained right now.

More soon.

Hugs to you.

Send some back.

Greg

It was the same from everyone: uncertainty as to where they would go, shock about the extent of the damage and loss, the certainty, as Greg so aptly puts it, that "New Orleans will never ever be the same" again.

The New Orleans of my pal Flashman stumbling obliviously through his life must now give way to a city determined to rebuild and reinvent itself.

Into what?

NEW ORLEANS: Not Big and Never All That Easy

New Orleans had one of the worst school systems in the country. People said that was by intent. How else could you keep a labor force willing to work for dirt wages cleaning the toilets and making the beds of the tourists coming down to make fools of themselves on Bourbon Street, overpaying for watered-down drinks, guzzling 64 ounce beers, showing their breasts, and generally trashing your home town?

In these pages, more than once, I've called New Orleans "the American Haiti." It is, now more than ever.

Former New Orleans mayor Mark Morial, now in charge of the National Urban League, watched the devastation on television like the rest of the country and told the various reporters interviewing him that the Crescent City reminded him of looking at Pompeii. The only difference was that this modern city was being overtaken by raging waters, while the ancient city had succumbed to a storm of molten lava.

The hometown football team, the New Orleans Saints, are moving to San Antonio for the time being. Locally, we always called them "the Ain'ts," anyway.

Early today, Wednesday, Mayor C. Ray Nagin was airlifted from City Hall, where he had manned his post throughout this crisis, as rising water began to assault that structure, as well. Meanwhile, the bus convoys were taking the citizens of his city off to the Houston Astrodome. Nagin said that he was concerned about the disease that would come from the corpses left floating throughout the city. "We know there is a significant number of dead bodies in the water," and "other people dead in attics," Mayor Nagin said. Asked how many, he said: "Minimum, hundreds. Most likely, thousands."

Meanwhile, among the chattering classes in service to the Mouthpiece Media, you had "pundits" like Jeff Jarvis (BuzzMachine.com) asking the insulting question: "Should New Orleans be Rebuilt?" I did respond to this blog post but tried to show equanimity in the face of this raging stupidity. (Who knows, I might need a reference from Jarvis one day.)

What? Is anyone asking if Biloxi or Mobile should be rebuilt? Why single out New Orleans again, you turd!

Why put New Orleans exactly where the Bush administration put New Orleans when the city asked for the help it needed to avoid a disaster EXACTLY LIKE THIS ONE? The Army Corps of Engineers went to the administration with a tin cup asking for a dollar to help keep people safe and their homes standing and the administration gave them twenty cents and said get lost.

Databases have been set up by CNN and a newspaper in Mississippi to help people locate lost loved ones in the aftermath of Hurricane Katrina and the flooding of the Crescent City. Any number of people have posted messages on the nola.com blog seeking elderly relatives they have not heard from since early Monday. That is one of the saddest parts of this whole debacle, in my view: the number of homebound seniors who could not get out of the city and who have no way of contacting anyone. I ran into a lot of older people like that in the Lower Nine. They would not have been able to get up to the rooftops of their homes, I know....

I met these people because, earlier this year, I worked as a community organizer in the lower Ninth Ward of New Orleans. The Lower Nine was an adjunct to the City of New Orleans. You had to cross the Industrial Canal to get there. It was your last stop before hitting St. Bernard Parish. It was predominantly black. The street conditions were abominable, akin to Haiti. The drainage was so bad that small children could actually swim on certain streets after a heavy summer rainstorm. Potholes were ubiquitous. Abandoned houses ran chock-a-block through the neighborhood, providing breeding grounds for rats, snakes and other pests. Wild dogs roamed the streets. Corner stores acted as fronts for drug dealers, and there were places along the bus lines going toward Florida Avenue where the roughnecks owned the block and flaunted their weapons and their crack deals.

The Lower Nine was forgotten and neglected - by design.

Part of the standard sales pitch I had to spiel to get people to sign away access to their checking accounts for the poverty pimp agency, ACORN, was, "Do you think you'd have these problems, these issues, if you lived on St. Charles Avenue?"

"Hell no!" was the usual and expected reply.

"Why not?" I was scripted to prompt them.

When we practiced our "rap" back at the ACORN office on Elysian Fields, we already knew the canned responses. There were usually only two of them.

"Because they're White" or "Because they got money."

In a CNN interview today, the news reader, Daryn Kagan, said, "New Orleans is a racially engineered city, isn't it?" My jaw dropped. She said, "Weren't certain neighborhoods built for certain people to live in them?"

As we used to say in Nawlins, "Yes, indeed!"

During the four years I lived, worked, and played in New Orleans with all my friends who have now become refugees, as I have always been, I can recall reading at least seven major articles in the Times-Picayune about the problem of getting federal funds to keep the city, already below sea-level and prone to flooding, from washing away. According to the article in Editor and Publisher and Amy Goodman's reporting for her radio show "Democracy Now!" the local New Orleans paper brought this issue up even more times than my memory serves.

The point of the articles in that newspaper was that one day the Big One that overwhelmed the levees and pumping system would come and that action could and should be taken in advance to avert a catastrophe. All that was required was providing the funding that SELA was created to utilize, and the Army Corps of Engineer recommended, to make New Orleans safe.

All of this happened concurrent to George W. Bush being in the White House and pursuing his twin agendas of tax cuts for the wealthy and a misguided war and occupation in Iraq. I know. I was there.

Another writer has said that there are only three story cities in America: New York, San Francisco and New Orleans. Today, I suppose there are only two.

The Bush administration should be held accountable for the death of a great American city.

As this disaster unfolded and everyone else in the country was suddenly talking about the city that had been my own special obsession for the last four years, I came back to say this on the Web:

LIZARD LICK, North Carolina 3 September, 2005

It's Labor Day weekend in America. It's a time when people throw things on the barbecue, invite friends and loved ones over, and generally get ready for a new school year or semester. The last holiday before the serious Holy Days rush that comes as winter approaches. Labor Day, in America, has always been a time when the dignity of work was acknowledged. It is that time when the average person, the regular guys and gals jumping into their cars in the early morning, are seen as a definition of something everyone could believe made the nation whole.

But not this weekend. This weekend is the culmination of the five days that have defined the future of America and the presidency of George W. Bush.

The President of the United States did not do the traditional Saturday radio address on this Saturday of the Labor Day weekend. Instead, he appeared on live television to assert--unequivocally--that the city of New Orleans will be rebuilt. Then, having finished his prepared statement, he rushed toward the door back into the White House. A reporter yelled out, "Mr. President, why did it take so long?" Meaning for our government to respond to the crisis.

Mr. Bush looked grim. He threw a hand into the air and kept on walking.

Figure 5: Flooding at the Ninth Ward Levee

Karl Rove, who is embattled himself, would have wanted the aftermath of 9/11 to be the defining moment of George W. Bush's presidency. Donald Rumsfeld, who stood beside Mr. Bush this morning during his statement to the nation, would most likely have wanted the "shock and awe" of invading Iraq to be the defining moment. Mr. Rumsfeld and his neo-conservative empire builders wanted the invasion to demonstrate to the world that it was time to march to the drumbeat of their new empire. But today, this Labor Day weekend, there is a growing sense that New Orleans, the disaster in New Orleans, is the defining moment of George W. Bush's presidency.

Anyone looking at Mr. Bush's face as he returned to the Oval Office this morning knows that George W. Bush knows that this is the defining moment.

"Shame, shame on America," said Representative Diane Watson, Democrat of California. "We were put to the test, and we have failed."

There were two cities of wondrous, historical architectural beauty in the United States of America--an ahistorical empire--one was Savannah and the other was New Orleans. Today there is only one.

The old buildings from the Spanish and the successive French regimes in New Orleans might have survived. But as we watched the looting of Baghdad's historical treasures on CNN television after the American invasion, we have now--during this five days that have changed the world--watched the looting of New Orleans.

Fires rage in downtown New Orleans as I write this. The Central Business District (CBD) and the adjoining French Quarter are shrouded by smoke.

As we reported here yesterday, there is a toxic chemical fire downtown. Bodies still float in the streets.

The woman my Web magazine's readers know as the Love of My Life sent a rant out to the rest of the world after reading what I have written about New Orleans, Katrina, and Bush.. She said this:

What I Understand

Consequent to the aftermath of Hurricane Katrina, I now understand, that the time to doze in the fat September sun, is over, that the time has come to stop participating in the personal and public hallucination that the United States government will, or can, help us, should natural disaster or warmongering afflict us the way it has already afflicted the southern states impacted by Hurricane Katrina.

That the 'greatest nation on earth' is not capable of providing succor to its own people, is a stark fact. The time to understand why and how this is true, is gone past. The time has come to realize, that it is only the 'us' of the U.S. who will help each other as much as help is possible.

Now we must consider which 'us' we belong to, and it may help to know, that in the blink of an eye, the enfranchised can become disenfranchised; that geographic distance is an illusion as far as what is possible here and now, for you and me, whoever you are reading this; that it matters little whose immigrant or native son or daughter you are, when the wolf is at your door. Considering that the whole country is built on stolen land, the privacy and ownership of what we have to lose is in the end, a moot point... ownership is also an illusion. Just ask victims of eminent domain... victims of Katrina, victims of decades of unscrupulous policy.

In the fat September sun, I already realize, I cannot really afford what winter will surely bring. I am 'buying time', on credit in some cases, just as our government has done. 'Buying time' is in itself, a concept that beggars reason; it is impossible, but we do it anyway. The bill will come due for us, en masse.

Now you may think regarding New Orleans, "Well, they should have never built that place like they did."..cold comfort I think; I don't feel I really have any control over, say, the development Route 12A in West Lebanon, or the traffic that backs up onto the Interstate at the Norwich exit., and I'm a reasonably intelligent person, with all my senses intact; how on earth would I demand that people born anywhere in the United States deserve to suffer and die because they cannot control the past or the policies of their government; I have no control over the smallest rudiments of the civic present. The present regime in Washington is proof of that.

We will buy oil or gas or electricity or wood to heat this winter, we will hope that our unborn children are vouchsafed a safe future, that the nursing homes which house our aging parents can afford to operate, that we can afford to drive to work every day, to a job that in some cases pays a living wage,

We will hope for the safe return of those number of us who are fighting a war waged for (at best) ambiguous reasons far away,

And we will start to understand I hope, that we are just like the 'them' we read about, right now, all over the world.

Separated only by the illusion of geographic distance, the accidents of birth, and the slightest tipping of the unfathomable scale of fate in our favor, right now, in the fat September sun, we are all in this together.

But have no illusion; the government of the United States, cannot, or will not help us, whomever 'we' are, should the wolf finally come to our personal door. At least, that is my understanding.

I found it ironic and touching that the woman I have most loved in this life should suggest, as she did in her opening paragraph, that people needed to step up, get off their duffs and make a contribution to their brothers and sisters in this world. Dang! I've been making that argument myself for years.

It would be nice to think that governments support their people but history has proved that is not the truth.

When I traveled to the inaugural in the capital of the empire in 2001, I had the sense that there was something rotten in America.

Marjorie Cohn, a writer for Truthout.org (yeah, another lefty site like mine) compared the empire's response to this catastrophe to that in Cuba at another time--that nation in this hemisphere we most vilify and maintain a senseless embargo against. Well, I have relatives in Cuba. I worry about them every day, just as I worry about my friends here.

Here's just a snippet of what Ms. Cohn said:

Our federal and local governments had more than ample warning that hurricanes, which are growing in intensity thanks to global warming, could destroy New Orleans. Yet, instead of heeding those warnings, Bush set about to prevent states from controlling global warming, weaken FEMA, and cut the Army Corps of Engineers' budget for levee and flood wall construction in New Orleans by $71.2 million, a 44 percent reduction.

Meanwhile, about Cuba, earlier, she wrote this:

After Hurricane Ivan, the United Nations International Secretariat for Disaster Reduction cited Cuba as a model for hurricane preparation. ISDR director Salvano Briceno said, "The Cuban way could easily be applied to other countries with similar economic conditions and even in countries with greater resources that do not manage to protect their population as well as Cuba does."

A friend and former Time magazine correspondent in Rome wrote that I was exposing the reality of New Orleans, as opposed to the popular fantasy that most non-New Orleanians harbor in their minds when thinking of Carnaval season and JazzFest. I thought I had been doing that over the last four years. I guess, up until now, no one was really listening. You don't know what you've got until it's gone.

To be just, I must admit here that many New Orleanians, despite the evidence of their own eyes, also believed in and helped promulgate the fantasy. Bon temps roulez. While watching breathtaking poverty, an inequitable plantation system of employment still thriving, neighborhoods of destitution and devastation cheek-by-jowl with gentrified condos that were unspeakably over-priced, as long as the bars were open and the couriers for the drug dealers kept delivering the cocaine and smack on time, everyone pretended that things were just fine and the Hell with the rest of America.

Like I said, the many thousands of body bags the parish had stored for a disaster worse than Katrina--if you can imagine that--were a local joke.

I appreciate the fantasy of New Orleans as much as the next person.

The New Orleans I knew was the closest thing to cosmopolitan, outside of Europe and Manhattan, that I had discovered in the United States. But it was also living in the shadow of the Jim Crow South. Racism was rampant, institutionalized and evident to anyone with the eyes to see. Mr. Bush carried that state because the Baptist coterie that rules outside of Catholic New Orleans plays the fiddle and controls the purse strings.

It was not surprising to me that NOLA mayor Ray Nagin said there should be a moratorium on press conferences. He was subtly speaking to a governor who looked more shell-shocked herself on CNN than helpful. And her only help was to hold out a plea for a real leader to deal with the situation in Mr. Nagin's city.

Figure 6: Dr. Bob creating a "Be Nice or Leave" sign.

In most New Orleans establishments, restaurants, tobacco shops, bars, you would see a sign, usually on carved wood, with the emblem, "Be

Nice or Leave." These signs were made by a local artist everyone knows as "Dr. Bob."

Dr. Bob was a former bar patron of mine when I was on the other side of the bar, a friend and one of my favorite raconteurs. He would often go off to Manhattan to visit a woman he loved and exhibit some of his serious artwork. Old Dr. Bob is a New Orleans fixture. If you lived anywhere near the French Quarter, you knew and had probably sat beside him as he had a few of his habitual lite beers. If you owned an establishment, you sooner or later bought one of his "Be Nice" signs because it was an emblem of our city.

I read on the nola.com blog a few days ago that Dr. Bob had taken to sitting around with his piece (that is one of his weapons) and had produced a new sign:

"If you loot, I shoot."

That is emblematic of what has happened to our city.

As I continue writing, my friend in Rome sends me a copy of an Associated Press story listing what landmarks, particularly in and around the French Quarter, are still intact. I want to write back to her, dear woman, that I'm more concerned about people than businesses or buildings. Yes, the structures are essential to what was New Orleans,but I tend to put people first. It was the people that made that city for me more than the architecture.

In the Associated Press story they don't mention anything on Frenchmen Street, in the Marigny, so I can only imagine what happened to The Spotted Cat where I was once a day shift bar manager/bartender. That was the bar where I had the longest tenure in New Orleans. This was during a time when most people felt that Frenchmen, especially for the locals and music lovers, was the street that Bourbon Street should have been. It was my habit, on a Sunday night, at the end of my shift, to give big tips to Jerry Jumanville's band to play "Harlem Nocturne" for me.

Jerry, a sax man, would ham it up no end on that piece, but I loved it anyway because I've always been a jazz lover. (For my money, Duke Ellington does the best version of "Nocturne.")

I remember when I lived in an apartment in the Treme, the oldest black neighborhood in the country, founded by free black people during a time when slavery obtained in most of the South. It was a place right out of the "Tales of the City" television portrayal of Armisted Maupin's book. It was right off Esplanade Avenue, that street so suffused with the scent of jasmine during the spring and summer. Just walking down that street during those seasons made you feel good.

It was while I lived in that place, still bartending at the Cat, that I had my one and only day of not showing for work on time. I had gone out dancing with a woman I ran into at the back bar in Molly's at the Market on Decatur Street, at the end of my shift the night before. She was wonderful. We went to play ping-pong at a bar on Royal Street and then danced late into the night on Frenchmen. I must have finally gone to bed about five in the morning. I missed opening the bar that Sunday and everyone assumed that I must be in the hospital or jail.

Thinking about my time at the Cat brings back the faces of people who lived in and loved New Orleans and what that city meant to us, my patrons, my friends. I see JW in my mind's eye, Ian, Mary, Scott, Matt, Dr. Bob, Sally Mae, Trish and Ed, Larone, Dave, Cheryl, Valerie, Beth and Fergus, and on and on... Faces of the habitues of the French Quarter who I've written about and for over the years. Now I must wonder if they survived this tragedy.

As I said, the President asserted that New Orleans will be re-built. But it will not be that same New Orleans. It will never, ever be the New Orleans I once knew. That city is gone. Many of the people who lived there will never return. They are building new lives for themselves as I write this.

So this book, I suppose, besides being a call to action to the national conscience, has also been my way of getting closure on this loss. It has been my way of getting the hurt and anger out of my system. What are the stages of accepting the death of something/someone you loved? Denial, Anger, Sadness, Acceptance? I have felt all of those while writing this.

All have washed through me except the anger. I am angry at my government.

It has been the agenda of the Republican party in the United States to dismantle the federal government for the last fifty-plus years. From Nixon to Reagan to Bush, the mantra has been, "get government off the backs of the people." The New Deal instituted by President Roosevelt was seen as the destruction of free trade and the market-driven economy. It had to go. On this Labor Day weekend, we can see in America that it has. We can see that there is no federal government to respond to the needs of the nation's people. New Orleans is like Haiti, Mississippi and Alabama are remnants of what they used to be, and Mr. Bush can only say, "This is unacceptable."

I say, "You reap what you sow."

This "unacceptable" situation, the death of a great American city and a region, Mr. Bush, is the direct result of your policies. You needed the money that could have saved American families to prosecute your war and occupation in Iraq.

So let's ask the Ronald Reagan Question: Is American better off today than it was four years ago?

Answer: Hell no!

This Labor Day weekend in America, we have much more to consider than in many such holidays past.

When, in the course of human events, a people find that their government no longer can maintain the common good, provide for the general welfare, maintain order and secure a prosperous future, it is incumbent upon that people to take action and seek a redress of their grievances. When faced with a bankruptcy of leadership, a fundamental disconnect with the lives of the average families on the street, a people--a nation--must assume the civic responsibility to set things right. When such a moment arrives, it is a defining moment for a people, for a nation.

We have reached that defining moment.

For the sake of ourselves and that of future generations, from whom we have only borrowed this stewardship, we must act as the conscience of our nation and our times.

THE NINTH WARD

NEW ORLEANS, Poland Avenue, 5 February, 2005

Conditions in the lower Ninth Ward of Orleans Parish must be among the worst in the country. I work in this area every day and find it difficult to believe that much of it can even, legitimately, be described as urban. Yet it is part--though a distaff part since it is across the canal and thus separated from the rest of the city--of the city of New Orleans. It has to be its most neglected part.

* Rare police patrols, thus higher crime and blatant drug dealing.

* Lack of street drainage so appalling in some places that children can swim in the pools left after a typical hard rain.

* Potholes in the streets that are more like actual craters.

* Abandoned houses falling into ruin and blight that serve as either crack houses or breeding grounds for rats on every street and most blocks of those streets.

* Vacant lots where weeds and vermin are allowed to thrive for months at a time.

* Woefully inadequate street lighting.

These are just the most obvious problems and issues I've discovered while walking the streets and talking to the people in the community here. I have a mind to produce a photo essay on the conditions in New Orleans Ninth Ward, if only to show you graphically how appalling they are actually .

Meanwhile, there is a high percentage of home ownership in the Ninth Ward. These people pay property taxes but the services those taxes are supposed to provide simply don't get delivered. The money goes elsewhere (St. Charles Avenue, Lakeview) where the residents just happen to be almost entirely white. That is one of the reasons New Orleans' Mayor, C. Ray Nagin, has a less than favorable rating among the black community here.

LIZARD LICK, 10 September, 2005

I know the Ninth Ward. It was my home before it went under water.

As everybody now knows, I wasn't just jiving when I lamented the deplorable conditions of my neighborhood. Today, as I write this, it is my people from the Lower Nine, as we called it, that are the most difficult to find. I am still asking about my friend and former co-worker Tanya, who owned a house in the Lower Nine and who was one of the joys of my life in New Orleans. Nobody I know has heard anything about her.

Figure 7: Two men wading through chest-high water.

Tanya and I used to ride the neighborhoods of black folk in New Orleans like two cops, eating in her car when we could catch a bite, trading stories about our lives, then going out onto the street trying to be community organizers for the poverty pimp organization called Louisiana ACORN.

We hated that damned job but we did it because it paid the bills, even though we knew were just promising people pie in the sky for our paychecks. The Louisiana ACORN philosophy was that people like Tanya and me had to hustle our brothers and sisters to give the organization access to those peoples' checking accounts. That way the organization could talk about how it was helping our people.

The thing was, no potholes got filled, no sewers were put in, no effort was made to make City Hall accountable, like we claimed the organization would do. Naw, we were too busy signing up more suckers--ehm! new members--every week so that we--and especially our bosses--could get paid, way too busy to be bothered with making real political change.

The sad part was that Tanya and I knew that ACORN was even gaming us. They knew that we actually cared about the plight of our neighbors in the Lower Nine. We thought that just maybe, while no one was watching at the office, we could make something a little better for folks. Saps, that's what we were.

It's been said of New Orleans that it was a city where you could see a church and bar on every other block. That was almost true, although there weren't as many bars once you crossed the Industrial Canal and dropped down into the Lower Nine. There were far more of those establishments in the upper Ninth Ward, an area that was more mixed racially, with your more genteel whites and an influx of gays who were gentrifying and taking over the Marigny after 2000.

The largest gay community in Louisiana was in those pastel houses of the Marigny closest to the French Quarter that were starting to rent for rates that rivaled San Francisco or Manhattan, even for half a double shotgun. The dividing line, for the most part, between blacks and whites--and for rental rates--was St. Claude Avenue.

When I first moved to New Orleans in the summer of 2001, all my young, white hipster friends would warn me not to linger too long near St. Claude Avenue in our part of the Nine at night, and definitely don't cross that line. That's where the real thugs and bangers hung, and you could get your ass hurt. This was more a myth reflecting the racism they were inheriting from New Orleans than a truth. I crossed St. Claude whenever I wanted. That dividing line held strong for most whites, though, up until the mid-oughts, when housing costs in the Marigny became so prohibitive that most poor people couldn't live there anymore. Then the gentrification started magically crossing St. Claude Avenue in the upper Ninth Ward, too.

The gentrification and de-blackification of the upper Nine was only starting to creep down toward Poland Avenue, your last stop before crossing the water to the Lower Nine, when I left New Orleans at the beginning of this summer of 2005.

I lived on Poland Avenue for a while then, helping renovate an apartment in exchange for the roof over my head. I used a five gallon paint bucket for a chair and a junk shelf that I found in dumpster for my desk. I slept on blankets thrown on the floor at night. It was at least a roof over my head and folks didn't say much about it since I had not that one job but two. The other one was organizing for ACORN before I was tasked to start trying to unionize the deputies of Orleans Parish Sheriff's Department. That's another story for another time.

Many of the more legendary bartenders of New Orleans, from the Quarter and Marigny, lived in the Ninth Ward. There was Bobby Lewis at BJ's down off France Street, Kathleen Hawes, who floated between The John on Frenchmen and Burgundy, the R Bar on Kerlerec, did a short stint at The Spotted Cat, all after her father sold the notorious and scandalous The Abbey on Decatur Street over in the French Quarter. Kathleen and I became friends from the moment we met, during her time at The Abbey.

There was Monica from The Apple Barrel. There was Lorelei who did stints at The Abbey, and Melvin's when she wasn't stripping. Sarah from historic Buffa's. Boo LaCrosse from Checkpoint Charlie's and later Lucky's.

And there was Jak Lynch, who most of us who were his intimates knew as "Naked Jak" because of his penchant for doffing his clothes-- when he wasn't behind the bar, of course. No, that happened when he was three sheets to the wind and loved the music he was hearing or the woman he was dancing with. Jak was once one of the best bartenders in the Quarter. But he got 86'ed (restricted from a bar) all over town. Whiskey was not usually a good thing for Jak. But when you had customers five deep, in other words when even the best bartender found himself "in the weeds," Jak Lynch was the man you wanted at your back. Jak, after years of working for Jim Monaghan, Sr., the owner of many New Orleans bars including the renowned Molly's at the Market, could sling drinks like nobody's business. Even though he hung in the Ninth, and was a true spirit of the place who everybody knew, Jak moved to the Treme a couple years before the end came for New Orleans.

When I got my job at The Spotted Cat, Jak said I was hired to replace him. That was not true.

From the Spotted Cat there was Daniel ("The Machine"), JW, and me. Being a bartender, most of the other service industry folks in New Orleans were quick to tell you, was being at the top of the food chain. In many ways it was, but it was no picnic. Those of us in the bartender family, sorority, fraternity--whatever you wanted to call it--would privately share the sentiment that most New Orleans bar owners were out of their minds. If you were lucky, you get an owner that was only mildly crazy and stayed out of your way and let you sling drinks. If you weren't lucky, you had to abide the real maniacs.

That's why I seldom talk about once being manager at Melvin's on St. Claude.

The Ninth Ward in New Orleans has suddenly become a focus for lots of what the babbling class, the punditocracy, has to say about America. From Michael Eric Dyson on the HBO program "Real Time with Bill Maher," aired Friday 2 September, 2005, to editorials in the Baltimore Sun, the San Jose Mercury News, the New York Daily News and elsewhere. As a former resident of the Nine, I can only find this ironic in the extreme. I can only ask, "Where were you, America?" before the Ninth Ward was devastated? Where were you when you knew that almost 100,000 of us living in the Ninth Ward made the official Poverty Index of our government look like describing what we would have called living good? Where were you when those body bags were ordered that everybody, at every level of government in this country, knew were primarily meant for us? Where were you?

These things were said on the Bill Maher broadcast that I referenced:

"The point is that these poor black people who were suffocating in poverty didn't just get suffocated in poverty when the flood came. It was before the flood." – Michael Eric Dyson

"There's an opportunity here. And hopefully, this will not just be about infrastructure and - for God's sake - having the National Guard at home guarding us as they should be. But it is an opportunity to look at the fact that there is structural poverty in this country that is getting worse." – Bradley Whitford

And here's one more quote that seems appropriate as I try to recreate for you the Ninth Ward that is lost to me, and America, forever.

"The responsibility of ministers for the public safety is absolute, and requires no mandate. It is in fact the prime object for which governments come into existence." -- Winston Churchill

"Ninth Ward!" a rallying cry

You had some kind of credibility (cred') in New Orleans if the people of the Ninth Ward would accept you. In local rap songs, "Ninth Ward!" was a rallying cry. There are a few reasons for that, some good, a lot bad.

From the Greater New Orleans Community Database:

The most noted artist to come from the Lower Ninth Ward is the legendary great, Antoine Domino, Jr., known as Fats Domino, the rock-and-roll legend. Although often performing in Europe, Fats Domino still lives in the Lower Ninth Ward with his wife Rosemary. His awards have been many, including the Grammy's Lifetime Achievement and Hall Of Fame Awards.

The Lastie family is one of the largest and most highly regarded musical families in New Orleans. Deacon Frank Lastie, family patriarch, played trombone and drums in Lower Ninth Ward churches. His sons, Melvin, David and Walter Lastie followed in their father's musical footsteps and became accomplished musicians in their own right.

Kermit Ruffins spent his childhood years in the Lower Ninth Ward, attending the area's public schools. Kermit is an internationally known trumpeter, vocalist and bandleader. He co-founded the Rebirth Brass Band, leads his present band, the Barbeque Swingers, and occasionally performs with his "Kermit Ruffins Big Band."

The Lower Ninth Ward was among the very last of the city's neighborhoods to be developed. Bordered by the Industrial Canal to the west, the Southern Railway railroad and Florida Avenue Canal to the north, the parish line to the east and St. Claude Avenue to the south, isolation from the rest of the city and lack of adequate drainage systems contributed to its slow growth.

Originally a cypress swamp, the area was the lower portion of plantations that stretched from the river to the lake. Poor African Americans and immigrant laborers from Ireland, Germany and Italy desperate for homes but unable to afford housing in other areas of the city risked flooding and disease to move here. In the 1870s, several African American benevolent associations and mutual-aid societies organized to assist scores of struggling freedmen (formerly-enslaved Africans) in the area.

Although legislation was passed in 1899 for drainage and pumping systems, it was not until between 1910 and 1920 that the city installed adequate drainage systems, including the Jourdan, Tupelo and Florida Avenue Canals, in preparation for construction of the Industrial Canal. The Industrial Canal, built to connect the Mississippi River to Lake Ponchartrain, was completed in 1923, and further isolated the neighborhood from the city proper.

The lack of sewerage, continual drainage and water distribution problems did not deter desperate immigrant and African American workers from moving to the Lower Ninth Ward in search of a place to live and employment in nearby industries. The area continued to maintain a rural feel and the Lower Ninth Ward's reputation for neighborliness actually attracted some New Orleanians from other crowded city neighborhoods.

By 1950, only half of the Lower Ninth Ward had been developed. Industrial development during this time was along the dry docks of the Industrial Canal with a few scattered uses appearing in predominately residential sectors at the north end of the neighborhood. In the late 1950s, the second bridge between the city and the Lower Ninth Ward, The Judge William Seeber Bridge, known locally as the Claiborne Avenue Bridge, was built across the Industrial Canal at Claiborne Avenue. Retail development along St. Claude Avenue became notable during this period and the trend of corner stores continued. By 1965 commercial activity along St. Claude continued to grow and industrial development accelerated in the strip bordering the Industrial Canal between Claiborne and Florida Avenues. Scattered industrial and commercial uses throughout residential areas of the district continued as well. [Ibid.]

It always sounds dry when outsiders try to describe the place you live. They miss the music, the flavor of the cooking in the neighborhood is lost, and you don't see the old and young brothers sitting out on the stoop. You can't do that with just "information." It takes soul.

When Robin "Roblimo" Miller, my former editor at the former Andover News Network, now Open Source Technology Group (OSTG), and I first discussed this book, I joked about running into Fats Domino at the Winn-Dixie in the Nine.

Kermit Ruffins lived in the Treme at the edge of the Nine, where the Treme goes hard on the French Quarter, and he played at Vaughn's down in the Nine, near the Industrial Canal, every Thursday night he was in town rather than touring.

Figure 8: Fat's Domino's House in the Lower Nine

NEW ORLEANS, 28 January, 2002: Super Bowl

Like so many New Orleans writers before me, I'm composing this missive from a bar. I am working on a laptop computer, unlike my forebears, so I can write anywhere. Matt has sprung for drinks after we watched the Krewe of Barkus (dogs dressed as people) Mardi Gras parade down in the Quarter. We're sitting in a local bar called The Spotted Cat listening to another of the fabulous bands you get to hear in this town for free. The band is called Augie Jr. and The Big Mess Blues Band. We are waiting to see, as everyone in Nawlins is, which teams we'll be hosting next weekend for the NFL playoffs. Correction: we know that the New England Patriots are coming to town. As I write this we are wondering if the St. Louis Rams, who gave us that badass shellackin' or the Philadelphia Eagles, who we'd much rather have, will be coming.

Either way, it's on, Baby. Nothing but a wild party in The Easy for weeks to come. And we'll all pretend to get some work done along the way. Heh!

By the time Matt and I leave the bar and the great music behind, headed home to cook chili (more peasant food), it's all over for that playoff game except the crying. Mostly ours, as we shall get the Rams vs. the Patriots

As is the New Orleans Way, shortly after arriving home I get a call from the Kerry Irish Pub, confirming that I shall be available to work the door for both Super Bowl and Mardi Gras. (No sane man would agree to do this, of course, but when you're deeply in debt err' job is better than ne'er job, as the old timers used to say.) Besides, there won't be (much) of a conflict with my new job, which is nearby. I'll just have long days on Mondays and Fridays, when the best plan will be to stay in the French Quarter for a quick sandwich between jobs. With any luck, some of the other staff will kick down a few tips .

And that's part of the New Orleans Way, too: complete dependence on the behavior of people from somewhere else. Smile and shake your money-maker.

Here's another example. In the office where I work my new Day Job on Bourbon Street, we are sitting right on stage, for all intents and purposes, because the band that plays in the club next door--and usually kicks in between 3:00 and 4:00 in the afternoon--is on the other side of the wall between the bar and our office. You can hear this band a block away , so guess how it sounds to us?

It makes no sense complaining. The company I work for owns a group of restaurants and nightclubs on and around Bourbon Street. They're in the same business as the place next door, and are just as responsible as anyone else for making sure the revelers on that strip of excess stay fat and happy. Bourbon Street is where the well-heeled go out to play.

It's the New Orleans Way that the young, boho, hipster set--all tattoos and dark clothing--hangs out on Decatur Street, rather than Bourbon, and look down their cocaine-frozen noses at Bourbon and all who go there. Coke's not the only drug to be found in the haunts of Decatur

Street, of course. Heroin and pot are plentiful enough, and neither they nor crack go short of users in New Orleans. I've seen more people go into nods in the middle of conversations here in New Orleans than any place I've ever lived. That's one of the reasons I've told Matt I've got to leave Casa de Caca: roommate number three nods more than not and I don't like putting up with that crowd.

The hipster set's favorite places on Decatur are called The Hideout and The Abbey, but you'll find them hanging out at Molly' at the Market as well. (The name comes from the famed French Market near the river.)

They also frequent places like the Hi-Ho, the Shim Sham, and The Morgue. (The names tell almost the whole story, don't they? Each place is a bit more seedy and disreputable than the next.) Caio (roommate #3 at Casa de Caca) likes the Hideout a lot. It's full of people who don't mind the fact that the place usually reeks of vomit.

That's the New Orleans Way.

But let's end on a positive note! IF you're comin' to Nawlins for either Super Bowl or Mardi Gras, you MUST make it out to Miss May's located in the Uptown area. Miss May's is located on the corner of Magazine Street and Napoleon Avenue right across from the cop shop (police station). It's open 24/7, as you'd expect, and is a good neighborhood bar--even though it's near Loyola and Tulane, not in the heart of the French Quarter.

Here's the Good Part: Well-drinks are only a dollar. Any time. All day. Great place to have a cheap date or just get your buzz on for cheap. That means you have to leave the French Quarter (clip joint) and its environs. You'll be glad you did.

NEW ORLEANS, 6 Feburary, 2002

Walking to and from work each day, I pass through the Fauberg Marigny ("the Marigny") and the French Quarter ("the Quarter"). At this time of year, many of the balconies and a number of the houses are festooned with banners, bunting, flags, and tinsel, all in Mardi Gras colors (purple, green and gold.) Some houses have carnaval masks larger than life, usually also in the colors, and you can see harlequins and manikins on the balconies in suspended states of revelry. It's a nice touch, found only in New Orleans.

Figure 9: Carnival masks in a curio shop window.

When I ask a local vendor or two who I have met at my office, suburbanites to a person, who live in Metairie, Jefferson or Gretna, they remember that there's a story around the colors, but can't tell me what that story might be or what the colors stand for. They suggest I look it up on the Web.

Before doing that, I decide to ask Matt, my roommate, who has steeped himself in New Orleans lore. Matt says that there's a love story, the details of which he was vague about at the time, in which a Russian prince--whose colors were purple, green and gold--was supposed to come to New Orleans to meet his lady love for Carnaval. But, because of a tragedy, the lovers were never to rendezvous. It apparently became a firestorm story for this city of "romantic warriors," and the colors were adopted. That's Matt's version.

The version I found on the Web says:

"Rex selected the official Mardi Gras colors in 1872. The 1892 Rex Parade theme Symbolism of Colors gave meaning to the colors: purple represents justice; green, faith; and gold, power.

"It's interesting to note that our Mardi Gras colors influenced the choice of school colors for arch rivals Louisiana State University and Tulane University. When LSU was deciding on its colors, the shops in New Orleans had stocked up on purple, green, and gold material for the Mardi Gras season. LSU decided upon purple and gold, and bought much of it. Tulane bought much of the only remaining color -- green! (Their colors are blue and green.) Remember to wear Mardi Gras colors whenever you're not in costume."

Nowhere near as romantic a story there, so I looked elsewhere.

In the book New Orleans, by Bethany Ewald Bultman (Fodor's Compass American Guides), you can read this:

"...There is much debate as to whether the first formal parade was held in 1835 or 1838, but no matter, the parades that traversed the muddy streets are said to have been wicked and satirical. The first krewe to parade was the Mystick Krewe of Comus (see "Krewes," p. 166).

Much of the pomp employed by the old krewes comes from the entertainments planned in 1872 when the Russian Grand Duke Alexis Romanoff came to New Orleans at Carnival time in hot pursuit of actress Lydia Thompson. Forty businessmen got together and founded the Krewe of Rex, mounting a daytime parade in the archduke's honor. Every Rex from 1888 to 1997 has belonged to the exclusively white and male Boston Club. The city's upper-crust folks, always socially ambitious, decided to adopt the Romanoff household colors -- purple (signifying justice), green (faith), and gold (power) -- as the official Carnival colors. The local gentry also learned that the Grand Duke Alexis's favorite song was a regrettable ditty called "If I Ever Cease To Love" from the New York musical Bluebeard that starred Ms. Thompson. All these years later, it remains the official song of Carnival. (The song is indeed so forgettable that many a jazz band gives up on the melody and plays a tune akin to "Little Brown Jug.")

Ahh! Matt came correct once again! AND besides the tales of pirates, future Presidents, the Spanish and then the French and Acadians here in New Orleans, we now have a Russian prince to add to the mix. Only in New Orleans.

You've all seen the Spanish architecture, with the wrought-iron balconies and fine courtyards, that characterize the "French" Quarter. They are special to this place, rivaled only by some of the fine architecture in South Florida as exhibits of some of the great work of that era.

Which is probably the best segue I can think of for our next point about the New Orleans Way: If you have money to spend, we have thousands of ways for you to spend it down here in New Orleans. From the curio shops and galleries to the ghost tours and great events like JazzFest, not to mention Mardi Gras, of course, the music, the foods, the restaurants and bars.

And this weekend, the Super Bowl, number "XXXVI" (36), is here in The Big Easy, too! This has disrupted much of our traditional Mardi Gras and caused some local animosity toward the National Football League, but many others have beaten that horse so I won't .

Let's just say that this week in the Quarter the beer trucks have tandem crews and have to jockey with the liquor distribution trucks for the commercial parking enforced in the Quarter every day until after 11:00 p.m.

I have a funny parking enforcement story for you. Matt's boss at the real estate office manages a building here owned by Gennifer Flowers. Yes, the same Gennifer Flowers notorious for being one of former President Clinton's bimbo eruptions. Ms. Flowers also performs at a dinner club here about four doors down from my office. It seems that Ms. Flowers is having guests in town for Mardi Gras and Matt was asked if he would do her the favor of moving some extra furniture to her place near Jackson Square.

While he is moving the furniture into the building with the assistance of a brother called Peanut, one of our ever-vigilant meter maids gave

Matt a citation. He was upset, because he was loading furniture in a loading zone. He was unaware, I explained, that in order to even stop in those zones during certain hours you needed to have the special "PRIVATE" plates given commercial vehicles. It was not the activity involved that mattered, but the taxes paid for the privilege. My explanation did not make him feel any better about the citation.

It was evident by this past Thursday that our town was totally into the giddiness of Super Bowl madness. Lots of the shops in the Quarter and along Canal Street -- that huge strip of three lanes in each direction and an island in the middle where cable cars run for the tourist trade, that strip capped by Harrah's Casino and featuring a number of major hotels, that separates the French Quarter from the Central Business District (CBD)--also offered Super Bowl memorabilia.

My boss's Super Bowl tickets arrived on Thursday, too. They are done up with one of those holographic strips that will make people want to keep and frame them. Each ticket cost him almost twice what I take home in a week...

By 2:00 p.m. Friday afternoon, from the Bourbon Street window of the storage area behind my office, I could see all of the "amateur" drunks (as we say here in Nawlins when we talk about tourists and suburbanites who come to town to drink) milling up and down Bourbon with large cups of beer clutched in their hands or leaning over the balconies of the noisy clubs boisterously calling down to the street, "Show your tits!" and then a huge roar of approval. I could only imagine what the crowds cruising the Quarter would be like by 8:00 p.m. when I was scheduled to clock on duty at the Kerry Irish Pub.

I cringed and went back to editing documents for my boss. The first band on the other side of the wall to our office was already blaring. This act would go on until about 4, when they would be replaced by a "party" band. The street was ready for a party band by that time. When I went outside to have a cigarette, I watched three drunken guys in business suits, one of them festooned with Mardi Gras beads, wrestling with each other like they were back in high school. Three sheets to the wind and the fourth one flapping... I turned to be buzzed back into our offices.

The convergence of Super Bowl and Mardi Gras is a dangerous mix. The best I can do is hope that I and all my friends in the service business of New Orleans make lots of money during the next two weeks.

And in the Middle of All This, an Election

We had a mayoral election here in the Big Easy on Saturday. Out of the fourteen candidates in the race, only two made the runoff: Former Police Chief Pennington and a "businessman" from Cox Cable named Nagin. Both are connected, one way or the other, to our outgoing mayor, Mark Morial.

Politics New Orleans-style is a nasty business, as you might imagine. I had that notion driven home to me last week. When the telephone rang, I picked it up, only to immediately be assaulted by a recorded female voice telling me not to vote for Mr. Nagin because he was a pawn of the Morial "machine." The female voice on the recording hit me with a stream of vitriolic accusations against Nagin and then the telephone call ended. No ascription, no endorsement of a particular candidate. Just two or three minutes of sound-bite venom. I've been around politics a long time now, but this was the first time in my life I've ever gotten a telephone call like that one anywhere.

The next day, Matt got the same type of hit-call about mayoral candidate Paulette Irons. Again, no ascription, no endorsement.

When you bring up politics to most people in this town, they cynically rejoin that nothing ever gets fixed but New Orleanians still get the best politicians that money can buy. Ha-ha!

Holding an election on Super Bowl weekend--something that couldn't have been anticipated when the election date was originally set--may have had a dampening effect on voter turn-out. But in a race with this crowded a field, a number of the candidates got more exposure than in races in other metros I've known. There was a definite small-town feel to the whole affair, with even the minor candidates getting a chance at many of the forums. That's the best thing I can say about an otherwise tawdry race where the word "Liar" was in no small evidence.

None of the rhetoric, accusations or mud-slinging managed to fill a single pothole in a city as plagued by them as any I've ever seen. The schools didn't get better in this quintessentially illiterate town, and the crime rate didn't drop one bit. The job market is still abysmal outside of the "hospitality" sector where most people work for minimum wage or less. Wait staff, bartenders, etc. still make $2.85/hour plus tips now that this election is over. That's the New Orleans Way.

I count myself lucky to have gotten a second "steady" job as a janitor at one of the local watering holes. I start that job right after the Mardi Gras festivities. I'll go in there at 5 a.m. and clean floors and toilets before going to my main Day Job at 9 and working until 5 p.m. One pal of mine says, "That's the way you've got to do it to make it in this town." He's lived here all of his life, so he should know...

What happened at the Kerry during Super Bowl weekend for me?

It went like this:

Got out of my Day Job at 7, with only an hour remaining before I had to clock in at the Kerry, I decided to go over early and check the lay of the land. It was incredibly quiet compared to the raging madness that was Bourbon Street. Looked like it would be a chill gig--at least at that moment--as Decatur St. was still slow. Mostly strollers, a few people lowing over pints, but nothing like the street party I had just left at my first job. That was good news. I ordered a Coke and waited for the long night to commence...

It was a long, dead night. I made $15 for staying there until 12:30 p.m. The explanation for the gouge isn't worth the ink. Let's just say it was another exhibition of the New Orleans Way. I have this bad habit of expecting people to be as concerned about keeping their word(s) as I am. My bad.

And the beers? I asked for one, to make the switch from the caffeine of Coca Cola to something mellower, bored as I was, and I got the message, "The bar says 'No. Not yet.'" Rule Two broken in keeping to the terms of a deal. But I felt duty bound to work the night, perhaps the weekend, out. That's me.

I decided to wait for Saturday. That turned out to be my best night of the weekend. I made $30.

Sunday went almost exactly like Friday and I made the same amount of money. I suggested that they might not need me during Mardi Gras weekend. I agreed to let them give me a call after they saw how it went on Friday. I'm disinclined toward ever going back there to work. Do the math. I made the equivalent of $2/hr. Fat Tuesday looms and things are supposed to pick up for the service workers in this town. This is The Season in New Orleans, I've been told since I moved here after leaving Belgrade in July. People are supposed to make all kinds of fat bank.

At my Day Job today I overhead some of the Bourbon Street business crowd beginning to sing the blues. The tune went like this:

Super Bowl weekend was "okay," some people did "alright." But it was nothing to write home about. One guy said he'd checked with the hotel crowd and heard that nothing much was going on today or tomorrow. That, in part, because any person with half a brain wouldn't fly into this town until after the airport reopened from the Super Bowl lock-down. (The only things in the air over New Orleans on Sunday were the fighter jets that scrambled when former President Bush came out to do the coin-toss.)

The assembled were wondering if the Mardi Gras krewes would reschedule their parades tonight as we are in the midst of a rainy cold-snap right now -- after having a great and unseasonable week before the Super Bowl, the krewes who normally parade having canceled therefore.

It's not just me, Kids.

New Orleans can't catch a break.

There are a number of major krewes scheduled to begin parading tonight and throughout Fat Tuesday. But if the weather doesn't break...

Losing My Religion

Let me tell you more about this Mardi Gras celebration. This is my first, so until now I only had anecdotes from people who have come here before me to rely upon. The big difference between their perspective and mine is that I have to live and work here; I didn't fly in to have a raucous party.

I'm not that into rampant debauchery, being older. My feelings about the upcoming festivities are mixed. It won't be any fun leaving an office on Bourbon Street and trying to make my way home, for example.

I have very little incentive to stay up 'til dawn with a bunch of college-aged revelers. Though I'm interested in absorbing what this newest of my cities has to offer, I've never been a good tourist.

I'm still thinking of this as merely a stop on the longer hejira. It seems that I shall stay here longer than I've planned, paying old debts from the last jaunt and collecting acorns for the next.

Oddly, at least one confidante of mine here seems to believe that New Orleans is now changing me, accepting me and taking me to herself. This person says that I'm even being taken by and taking to New Orleans faster and easier than my roommate, Matt, who loves this place.

Here's the impression: "Matt tries too hard to be part of New Orleans. He's not from here, but goes out of his way to act like he could be. That's not how it's done in New Orleans. You can't just take the place, the place has to take you.

"I've seen more people like you, Rod, who say they hate New Orleans, become part of this city than people who love it so much that they try to take the place.

"It ain't a place to be taken. It takes you, not the other way around.

That's why I think that, of the two of you, you're the one New Orleans will take and make you like her...."

I was nonplussed by this assessment, since Matt insists that everyone he likes should just move down here. Me, I'm taking to New Orleans, but from arm's length. Even more surprising is that this assessment came from someone I considered one of my roomie's friends and admirers. I thought the person was in league with Matt to make me like this town. It turns out that was not the case; the town has to like you first.

LIZARD LICK, 10 September, 2005

Living in Ninth Ward in New Orleans was no picnic. It took grit to live there and grit to find any kind of job in the adjoining, tourist-oriented French Quarter, which was what most of us--if we were motivated to have jobs--knew we had to do to survive. And it was about survival. Nobody was "living large," as the saying goes.

LOCKED DOWN

There was one other major irritant to life in the Ninth Ward, particularly the Lower Nine, that we all had to deal with: Transit out. There were three major barriers to getting out of the Ninth Ward and into the rest of the city. The first two should be obvious: The bridges that crossed the Industrial Canal. If the drawbridge on St. Claude Avenue was up and railroad bridge was closed because of a train, the Lower Nine was effectively locked down. People complained about this all the time and pressed the City of New Orleans to do something about it because all of the medical care was across the Canal, most of it clustered down at the Tulane Complex in the Central Business District (CBD.) There was a medical facility before they hit the third barrier, a train crossing near the switch that bisected that part of the Ninth Ward above Montague Street, the Bywater Hospital, but most locals considered that place a death trap. People would bleed in an ambulance being letting themselves be checked in there.

And there's that third barrier. The train would stop there, effectively closing down St. Claude Avenue and the adjoining streets. If you were lucky enough to jump off St. Claude and drive parallel to the tracks, you might make it Royal Street where you could cross over before the train had finished its business. That is, if you didn't get locked into a traffic jam on St. Claude after the train had already stopped. If that happened, you had to wait it out like everyone else. The train would back up after a while, make its switch and then move forward again until it was cleared to proceed. This entire process would leave you at a standstill for up to twenty minutes. If you lived in the Lower Nine, you knew there were certain times of day when you must simply add this additional obstacle to your travel time.

These three obstacles made life especially difficult for the elderly and the sickly.

That's what life was like, not just for me, but for many of the service workers--dishwashers, bartenders, bar backs, waitresses, and hotel maids who worked at those highrise hotels like the Marriot, Sheraton or Astor Crown Plaza on Canal Street. Our jobs were in the Marigny, the French Quarter, and the CBD but we could damned well not afford to live up there.

We could only afford to pay rents or--if we got lucky and saved--buy houses in the Lower Nine. We were the servants of the city that would rather have had us just gone.

And now we are gone. The Lower Nine is gone. Katrina took us out and Rita appears to have driven the nail in our coffin. The levee broke in the Lower Nine again and the water went back up to eight feet …

FEMA, HOMELAND SECURITY, AND THE BLAME GAME

LIZARD LICK, 10 September, 2005

The loss of New Orleans, as I've said, is about politics and government policies. There is no doubt about that. My close personal friends would still have homes and jobs if the governments to which they paid their taxes and who they trusted to care about them had been able to do the job we had all expected.

America failed us.

The Washington Post reported in a story from Spencer S. Hsu ("Inside FEMA -
Leaders Lacking Disaster Experience") on Friday, 9 September, 2005:

Five of eight top Federal Emergency Management Agency officials came to their posts with virtually no experience in handling disasters and now lead an agency whose ranks of seasoned crisis managers have thinned dramatically since the Sept. 11, 2001, attacks.

FEMA's top three leaders -- Director Michael D. Brown, Chief of Staff Patrick J. Rhode and Deputy Chief of Staff Brooks D. Altshuler -- arrived with ties to President Bush's 2000 campaign or to the White House advance operation, according to the agency. Two other senior operational jobs are filled by a former Republican lieutenant governor of Nebraska and a U.S. Chamber of Commerce official who was once a political operative.

Meanwhile, veterans such as U.S. hurricane specialist Eric Tolbert and World Trade Center disaster managers Laurence W. Zensinger and Bruce P. Baughman -- who led FEMA's offices of response, recovery and preparedness, respectively -- have left since 2003, taking jobs as consultants or state emergency managers, according to current and former officials.

Because of the turnover, three of the five FEMA chiefs for natural-disaster-related operations and nine of 10 regional directors are working in an acting capacity, agency officials said.

As our nation begins to focus on why New Orleans was lost, we have to wonder about those agencies we pay to protect us from terrorist attacks and other disasters and how competent their people actually are.

Unfortunately, if we really believe the evidence of our own eyes, we have to accept that what used to be our government is not driven by rational considerations of our needs as a people any longer. It is driven by an agenda, an ideological agenda.

On 6 September, 2005, in the New York Daily News, Juan Gonzalez reported:

All last week, FEMA bureaucrats gave prominent placement on the agency's Web site to Operation Blessing, the Virginia-based charity run by controversial right-wing evangelist and Christian Coalition founder Pat Robertson.

Back in 1994, during the infamous Rwandan genocide, Robertson used his 700 Club's daily cable operation to appeal to the American public for donations to fly humanitarian supplies into Zaire to save the Rwandan refugees.

Gonzalez goes on to report that it brings up the Rwanda effort because the refugees in that country never got the money. Instead, the funds were used to finance a business venture for Robertson in Africa. The televangelist was later indicted for the fraud in the state of Virginia, from where he broadcasts his television program "The 700 Club." I decided to check out his program when I learned he was raising money for victims of Hurricane Katrina. What I found was that the focus of his fundraising was on white evangelicals who never went anywhere near the Ninth Ward of New Orleans. What I found made me seethe.

But the Federal Emergency Management Agency (FEMA) lists Robertson's Operation Blessing as the third place to which people should send funds, supposedly to help my people in New Orleans.

That smells a lot like a damned political payoff to me.

I have to apologize to you, Gentle Reader, but I'm not feeling very trusting today and I'm certainly not feeling very secure.

If what happened to New Orleans is any example, nobody in America should feel very secure today.

The Southland Times, of New Zealand, looked at what happened and wrote in an editorial published 10 September, 2005:

Baghdad endured Operation Shock and Awe, a go-gettem invasion. New Orleans endured Operation Sloth and Chore, a screamingly lethargic and trudging official under-reaction to urgent humanitarian need.

Perhaps it's really not such a contrast. Maybe these two cities, in their writhings, were treated in an entirely evenhanded way by the same stiff and judgmental part of the American psyche that stampedes to protect money and assets, but also adheres to the belief that people who don't accept personal responsibility for themselves will oftentimes just have to suffer the natural consequences.

Remember that promptly after the invasion, United States troops put a ring of steel, fully 50 tanks, around the Iraqi oil ministry building and then watched, inert and passive, while all around them fell into chaos.

People killed one another to settle old scores, looted stores and museums, and ransacked Government buildings whose contents and records were important for any stable, functioning society to continue.

Only when the criticism from the rest of the world became especially pointed did the invaders--sorry, liberators--start to police the country over which they had assumed nominal control.

Those Iraqis dismayed at the way the U.S. presided over the descent into bedlam must now be reassuring themselves that at least it was nothing personal.

U.S. officials have shown pretty much the same indolence and neglect of the human suffering among many of their own citizens in the aftermath of Hurricane Katrina.

The forecasted warnings of hurricane damage could scarcely have been plainer: "Devastating damage expected ... most of the area will be uninhabitable for weeks ... water shortages will make human suffering incredible by modern standards."

Nothing unclear about that little lot. But what was the official reaction? Everyone get into your cars and get outta there.

Because everyone in that part of the US who's worth a damn has a car, right? In the land of personal responsibility, those without the sense or capacity to haul ass were left to fend for themselves.

Days came and went before it dawned on those authority figures who watched TV that the real scope of the problem was bigger than they'd figured. So in went the National Guard, just in time to force those third world locals back from the buses so the 600 guests and staff of an exclusive hotel could climb on board.

Everyone repeat after me: RACE and CLASS. We knew all about those in the Ninth Ward long before Hurricane Katrina blasted into town.

The Baltimore Sun had a better way of putting it in an editorial published 8 September, 2005:

After Katrina fiasco, time for Bush to go
By Gordon Adams

WASHINGTON - The disastrous federal response to Katrina exposes a record of incompetence, misjudgment and ideological blinders that should lead to serious doubts that the Bush administration should be allowed to continue in office.

When taxpayers have raised, borrowed and spent $40 billion to $50 billion a year for the past four years for homeland security but the officials at the Federal Emergency Management Agency cannot find their own hands in broad daylight for four days while New Orleans and the Mississippi Gulf Coast swelter, drown and die, it is time for them to go.

Bear in mind that most of the words featured in this chapter are not mine. I am only recounting what other, more erudite, people in our nation were thinking immediately following the death of my city.

I bring up these reports because I suspect you will not hear much more reporting like this from New Orleans, especially after Hurricane Rita gave Bush administration officials a chance to forget Katrina and move "forward." Just as with the war in Iraq, the Bush administration is now moving to shut down all independent journalism about this disaster.

"Democracy Now!" (http://www.democracynow.org/) reported on 9 September, 2005:

The journalists who have been covering Hurricane Katrina have literally been risking their lives for the last week. Reporters have been stationed in and around New Orleans since the Hurricane hit and have tirelessly reported on the devastation to the city. Some journalists have expressed enormous outrage at government officials for their slow response. A few television reporters openly broke down on air as they report the horrific conditions and the desperation of victims. Reporters have witnessed the militarization of the city and are starting to feel the effects of the government crack-down on information gathering. FEMA is now rejecting requests by journalists to accompany rescue boats searching for storm victims. In addition, journalists are being asked not to photograph any dead bodies in the region. NBC News Anchor Brian Williams reported on his blog, that police officers had been seen aiming their weapons at members of the media. And a blogger named Bob Brigham wrote a widely read dispatch that the National Guard in Jefferson County are under orders to turn all journalists away. Brigham writes: "Bush is now censoring all reporting from New Orleans, Louisiana. The First Amendment sank with the city."

Earlier this week, Reporters Without Borders issued a warning about police violence against journalists working in New Orleans. They highlighted two cases – in one case police detained a Times-Picayune photographer and smashed his equipment to the ground after he was seen covering a shoot-out with police. In the second case, a photographer from the Toronto Star was detained by police and his photos taken from him when police realized that he had snapped photos of a clash between them and citizens who the police claimed were looters.

In a transcript of the on-air interview that was part of this report, we read:

AMY GOODMAN: Our guest, Tim Harper, of the Toronto Star, telling us what happened when he was covering New Orleans, and Jacquie Soohen of Big Noise films whose done a number of films around the world, spent a good deal of time in Iraq covering the invasion and occupation and the time before. Jacquie, you just flew in late last night from New Orleans. Tell us about your experience there.

JACQUIE SOOHEN: Well, the experience with the police was two days ago. We were filming in the Ninth Ward, which is one of the more dangerous areas, supposedly, but also one of the hardest hit areas, and one of the areas where a lot of rescue operations haven't gone into, especially the Lower Ninth Ward. And we were just on the edge of that and we were filming with another photographer and a journalist. Curfew was approaching, but it wasn't quite there yet, and we had gone about the city at the same time of night, other times. And all of a sudden, out of nowhere, literally, there were four SUVs and a Humvee pulled up, and without any warning, D.E.A., Border Patrol, Louisiana Police Department and National Guard forces came out with their guns raised, pointed at our heads, and said, "Looters will be shot!" And we just began yelling as fast as we could, "We're press! We're press! We're press!" And I had my camera in my hand while that was going on. And they kept yelling at us, "Looters will be shot!" for -- this went on for a little while.

AMY GOODMAN: Were you with a resident of the Ninth Ward?

JACQUIE SOOHEN: We were with a resident of the Ninth Ward, who was also okay. We were all okay in the end. We talked them down. We were able to tell them we would just leave as quickly as possible, they also wanted to make sure that the resident of the Ninth Ward left. He was planning on staying, but they wanted to make sure that he left with us.

And I think what we did was we experienced more than anything, I mean, martial law as it was being enacted upon the city and the fear that it was causing in all of the residents, and the very next day, there were—I got two more phone calls from residents who were inside, who had suddenly decided to leave because they said they were being harassed and intimidated by the police, being searched on street corners, having guns pointed at them.

It's the old game of no bad news—especially not from the Ninth Ward of New Orleans, where my people lived.

More importantly, though, the bottom line on all this, what we learned watching people on rooftops in Nawlins, seeing Jefferson Parish President Broussard cry on national television, hearing the replays of Ray Nagin going off on radio, is that our notion of a Department of Homeland Security that might actually keep us secure in a disaster was a damned joke. America is now exposed to the world as an inept and blowhard giant that can't protect or provide for its own people.

And people in places like Atlanta and Detroit and Cincinnati must have been chilled. Why? Because the message from the national government of the United States was clear: if you are poor, and especially if you are poor and black.....

By the weekend of 9-10 September, 2005, the Bush administration had its surrogates working overtime on the television babblefest, saying that it was all the fault of the local officials in Louisiana. They certainly needed to go after that uppity black bastard, Ray Nagin. Why didn't he use those school buses? Why didn't he have enough food for those folks at the Superdome? Why was he whining on the radio instead of doing something?

It was straight out of Karl Rove's playbook, if you knew anything about textbook political smears.

"And while we're at it, let's take care of that loudmouth coonass from Jefferson Parish, Walter Maestri, too! Whaddayasay, Boys!"

That's all I want to say about these people. You make your own determination. I decided to write this book to tell you about New Orleans.

THE HIGH LIFE

NEW ORLEANS, 27 April, 2005

When you go for long periods of time without any money at all or any food or cigarettes, when you do get that first dollar, that first meal, that first cigarette, it slips through your hands like water through a sieve. The world reaches out and pulls that dollar from your hands. Your stomach cannot get full. That cigarette burns faster than a wildfire through dry grass. Faster and hotter. And then it's gone, all gone.

No one will hire you because they smell the desperation in your sweat. It oozes out of your pores like lava down the side of a volcano. They have x-ray vision, like Superman, and see that you only have thirty-two cents in your pocket. No one wants to hire somebody who needs a job that desperately.

So you walk down the street until you find the next "Help Wanted" sign and you fill out the next job application. What the hell do they want to know what elementary school I attended for? Are they really going to go back and ask the principal what my Permanent Record (heh!) says I was like at age seven? I don't think so.

Sometimes it is difficult to avoid putting down that I attended Ashahola Elementary School in Cloudcuckoo, Montana. But I keep my sarcastic personality under control. I act as if these details of a life so distant as to be almost a fairy tale to me are crucial for the person doing the hiring. I allow the lie to go unchallenged.

I run into a woman I know on the street.

"Hey! Wassup?" she asks. "When did you get back to Nawlins?"

"Months ago. How are you?"

"Really? I haven't seen you until now."

"I've been avoiding the Quarter."

"Good to see you!"

"Good to see you, too."

"So what's going on? Where did you go?"

"Phoenix."

"Arizona? Oh wow! How was it?'

"Okay. Desert. Mountains. I've always liked the desert."

"But you're back in New Orleans. They always come back."

"Yeah, I guess."

"I've gottah scoot. Good to see you, though. Let's hook up for a drink sometime."

"Good to see you, too!"

"Later."

She pedals off on her bike, down Royal Street and away.

I wave good-bye. I'm sure I'll run into her in some bar weeks or months from now, again, if I'm still alive, if I'm still here. She didn't ask for a telephone number or an address, so I figure she's thinking the same thing. It was so good to see me that she didn't need to know how to stay in touch, after all.

I applied for every crappy job I could think of during my first week staying at Flashman's: dishwasher, construction laborer, cashier at a corner store, "kitchen help" in an Ethiopian restaurant, bar back, tinker, tailor, candlestick maker. No one called back. None of my friends called to make a referral. I was starting to feel miserable and hopeless. Homelessness, it appeared, was only days away. I figured I should start looking for a shopping cart....

New Orleans has one of the most interesting skies in the subtropical South of the United States. There are seldom stratus clouds, but the cumulus are lush and present on the days when there are clouds. The nimbus clouds usually come as signatures of the gods at the end of the good days. They wax pink or orange on the horizon; they hang over the river like ensigns. Nimbus can take your breath away when they want to, in conspiracy with cumulus clouds transforming into horses, ducks, the face of Charles Manson.

The cumulus clouds unload on the city in violent torrents of dark grey fury, accompanied by ear-splitting cannonades of thunder and lightning so close that your eyes go blind for an instant before you see the smoking tree split in half yards away from you. It doesn't just pour when it rains, it inundates, soaks, smothers, washes your pores clean and all the detritus down to the river, the legendary Mississippi of Mark Twain's wet dreams--beer bottles, half a po' boy sandwich, condoms, a tennis shoe, crotchless panties, the body of a guy stabbed last night--and then the sun blazes everything dry in fifteen minutes. Because the rainforest has been smitten away, replaced by avenues, boulevards, alleys, old renovated houses and ramshackle huts, the sun bears down, beats down, and leaves you breathless after only fifteen minutes.

The rain makes things cooler, we say in Nawlins. But that's only true for fifteen minutes. Your rain-drenched self is replaced by your sweating "like a pig" self again and you go on living for the next cooling rain. That's what we say. But it's just another version of how someone tells a story about New Orleans that you know is only a version and not to be relied upon.

You can't rely on a damned thing in this city and everybody knows it. Let the Saints keep on losing.

The key to survival in New Orleans is to stay away from the French Quarter, its throbbing heart of excess and decadence and debauchery, its field of ghosts who walk. The further away the better. In the Quarter, everyone is either a tourist hell-bent on getting a thrill from being unlike themselves at home or someone with a dark story they need to play out tonight.

Fig 10: An example of classic French Quarter architecture.

You are just the scenery to either of these actions. You are an extra in someone else's movie unless you have some dark action of your own to play out in public. Here's an example:

"Dude! You'll NEVER believe what happened to me last night!"

"Try me," says Rod.

"Well, I ended up at The Abbey, on Decatur?"

"Every one knows where The Abbey is. You said, 'ended up,' which means you were already loaded. If you went to The Abbey, that means you were lookin' for trouble and probably found it. Tell me something new."

"Do you always have to be such a cynical fuck?"

"It's my job."

"Fuck you."

"So what won't I believe? I'm in suspense."

"Asshole. I'll tell you anyway. When is your dinner gonnah be ready?"

"Half an hour. Tell away."

"You said you had beerage. So where's my fuckin' beer?"

"I'm not a bartender anymore. You know how to find a refrigerator, I think."

"Asshole."

"Thank you." As he walks off toward the 'fridge, I put the Blue Demon, the computer Matt is letting me borrow, into sleep mode. Not much more work getting done tonight, I figure.

He pops the top of the beer can. Takes a long gulp. "Ahh! Beer!"

"So?"

"So I guess I'm 86'ed from The Abbey"

"Because?"

"You know that bartender with the big tits?"

"How many females who get hired in Nawlins as bartenders don't have big tits? Five?"

"I'd kick your ass if you weren't supplying the beer right now."

"If you feel froggy, leap."

"Anyways, I made the mistake of switchin' from just having Buds to doin' a few shots of whiskey."

"Always a mistake, in your case."

"Yeah, I know. I gottah stop drinkin' whiskey."

"So you always say."

"Well, I tried to hit on her."

"Mistake number two."

"And she wasn't giving me any play..."

"Go figure."

"...and then she starts chatting up a guy at the other end of the bar. That really pissed me off."

"And your solution was?"

The last thing I remember is jumping over the bar, grabbing her tits and then stickin' my head under the beer tap and starting to guzzle beer straight out of the tap."

"You're kidding. Right?"

"No. I guess I passed out or got kicked out after that."

"It must have been a soft landing. I don't see any bruises or black eyes."

"That's what's so weird. You'd think somebody would have kicked my ass." He took another long gulp of my beer.

"Luck of the Irish. Thank God for small favors."

"Isn't your dinner done yet?"

"Let me check it." I'd gotten chicken leg quarters at the Magnolia Market at St. Claude and France. $2.99 for five pounds. They were baking in the oven. When I came back, I said: "It's about ready. I guess you're my dinner guest?"

"Fuckin' A."

"I'm flattered."

"Asshole."

"So you don't actually know you're 86'ed, since you blacked out."

"You'd 86 me after that shit, wouldn't you?"

"Most definitely, if I were still bartending. But I don't bartend at The Abbey. Considering their customers, your behavior was not that out of the ordinary."

"Are you being serious now or are you just pullin' my chain?"

"I'm serious. You won't know if you're 86'ed until you try to walk in the door again. You might have been 86'ed only for that one night. Like: 'Get the hell out and don't come back tonight.' But if you go in tomorrow and behave yourself, everything's cool."

"You know," he said. "I know people from your Spotted Cat days who still claim you were one of the best bartenders in New Orleans."

"They must have all been Miles Davis fans. Mixology is easy, it's the other stuff that takes work."

"And you're one of the few bartenders who I never fucked up around."

"It must be the grey beard. Makes people think I'm wise instead of the obvious: I've had a rough life."

"So you think I should try goin' back in The Abbey."

"The worse that would happen is that you'd learn you actually are 86'ed."

"Drunk or sober?"

"Your call. I'd keep in mind that bartenders have boyfriends, who usually aren't as forgiving as either bartenders or bar owners."

"That's what always has me worried. I walk into some place and everything's cool and then some bartender I pissed off walks in with her boyfriend and says, 'That's the guy!' and the next thing you know I'm munching a fist sandwich."

"Sound like a legitimate concern to me."

"Yeah," he nodded, guzzling more beer. "That's why I just stay in my apartment and pound beers. I figure I gottah lay low."

"Until you get a heat on."

"Yeah; until I get a heat on. Then it's out to any of the bars in the Quarter where I'm sure I'm not 86'ed yet."

"Last I heard there are over 200 bars in the French Quarter alone. Add in the Marigny and you've still got a few hundred places you can go and make an ass of yourself."

"Hey, you seen your buddy Matt lately?"

"Just the other night. His birthday was last week."

"He still with that crazy girl?"

"Jo? Yeah."

"Man, I don't understand that."

"Matt's always said he picks low-self-esteem broads."

"Why's he do that?"

"They worship any guy who'll spend time with them."

"You're sayin' he wants to be worshipped, right?'

[Our 'Applause' logo.] "Egads, Holmes! You astound me."

"Prick."

"You're confusing me now. I thought I was Asshole."

"But from what I hear, this woman ain't exactly worshippin' him."

"Far from it. She loves going negative, even with her man."

"Okay, so his plan doesn't seem to be working."

"Right again. But he's reached the age where it gets risky to change horses. He's never been very courageous, so it was easy for her to be the one getting worshipped. She trained him like a dog. I keep waiting for the wedding announcement."

"No lie?"

"No lie. Even men get scared in their mid-thirties. Been there. You actually start to accept that maybe you're with The Last Woman."

"I never think about shit like that."

"You're an exception. Most guys do, whether they admit it or not. Most of your friends are already married with children by that time. There's a lot of pressure, including from parents, to believe you should be, too."

"And what happens? You puss out?"

"Until you decide it's time for a train ride to Divorce City."

"That's bleak."

"This country has had a fifty percent divorce rate for nearly three generations now. You explain it."

"So this guy Matt, he's your best friend in New Orleans?"

"Rumor has it."

"But it was him made you quit your bartending job at The Spotted Cat, where they'd just given you a raise and everybody loved you?"

"Not exactly. It's a long story. He said he saw one of my co-workers stealing my tips, a guy I thought was a friend."

"And you believed him?"

"He's a lot of things, but I've never known him to be a liar."

"So you believed him and quit."

"That's the Reader's Digest version."

"Ever thought he might have wanted to sabotage your shit?"

"Not really. Let's move on to something else, okay?"

"And you can't go around his place because of the crazy woman?"

"You've got it about right. So what's your point?"

"Well, if this is your best friend, what are your enemies like?"

The question caught me off guard. I gave him five points in my personal tally for even asking. It's difficult to explain the ties that bind after knowing someone for a decade, to explain The Rules among men who are friends and compatriots (like NEVER, ever interfere in relationships), even harder to explain how you cut slack for men you've been through a lot with over the years. But the question did give me pause.

Cumulatively speaking, has knowing Matt caused me more harm than good? Probably. I could say that about a lot of people, though. A lot of people could say that about me...

I guess he could see the confusion his last question prompted in me.

"You got another beer, asshole?"

"Check the 'fridge. How should I know? How many have you had?"

"Here?" He wandered toward the back of my apartment. "You ready for one?" he called from the back.

"Why not?"

"Your chicken smells about done."

"Stick a fork in me, " I muttered to myself as he meandered back to the front of my place with the beers.

"You know, Rod, I really don't know why I do dumb shit like that. I mean, it's guaranteed to get either my ass kicked or 86 me from a bar I like to go to. I need to stop drinking whiskey."

"That's what you said."

He was earnest. "No! I'm serious, Dude. Beer is okay. But with whiskey I get off the hook."

"And the solution is?"

"I need a wing man."

"Come again."

"I need a buddy to go out with me when I'm drinkin'. Be my wing man and let me know when I'm not flyin' right. Like with those jet pilots?"

"Gotcha. I was thinkin' you thought someone should buy you buffalo wings after you had too many whiskeys."

"You're pullin' my chain, right? Don't answer that."

I didn't. I sipped my beer and waited for him to go on. It was time again for Rod's Confession Booth. I'd gotten used to these sessions since my first time living in New Orleans. People felt the urge to unburden themselves in my company.

"I know what it is; I need to find a way to put some meaning in my life, Dude. I just go from the drudgery of work to drinking, sometimes both at the same time, and back again. Nothing ever changes except the faces on the TV--and even those don't change that much. I don't feel like a single thing has happened in the last four years. Work, drunk, work, drunk, and then back again."

"Some people have a lot invested in seein' that nothin' ever changes in Nawlins," I observed. "I have a friend who's put it into one sentence: 'Let the Saints keep on losin'.'"

He snickered, then asked anxiously: "What is it about this damned place?"

"You tell me and we'll both know."

"People don't seem to want to get anything accomplished!"

Oh, things get done. It's just that the people doing them don't live in the parish. They all moved out to Kenner and Metairie and places like that long ago. Orleans Parish is just the place where the cheap labor force gets drawn from to keep the tourist businesses going. It's actually more profitable to have a basically under-educated and captive labor pool to change the sheets in the hotels and clean the toilets."

"So explain something to me, Padré."

"Padré? I remind you of a priest?"

"You remind everybody of a priest. Look how you live. You could turn a penthouse apartment into a monk's cell."

"What do you want explained?" I asked, after a sigh.

"Why did you come back here? You're obviously a smart guy AND a smart black guy. Why would you choose to come back to this hell-hole when there are so many better places you could be? You don't have a wife, kids, anything to keep you anywhere. Why come back to New Orleans when this place has always treated you like shit?"

Oh-oh. The bastard was trying to change chairs in the Confession Booth with me. We don't play musical chairs in Confession. "Valid question. Honestly?"

"No. Lie to me."

"I have friends and a support system here. And I have no place else to go."

"That's sad."

"No lie. I can see how it's breaking your heart.

"I think about it every night when I wake up at three in the morning. I don't have family, like most people. I'm eccentric as hell. No lovers, no ties to anything except my damn computer and the magazine. I call it orphanage.

"I'm not in New Orleans because I want to be. I want to be in Manhattan again but I can't afford it. So I run back here.

"I'm not getting younger. I'm certainly not the man I was at thirty-five. Most employers look at the missing teeth and the grey beard and decide I've already been used up. My resumé works against me in that potential employers think I'll want too much money. I have a good rep' here as being a primo house painter. When push comes to shove, since there's always a house being renovated somewhere in the parish, I can just go back to being Manuel Labore and have a beer at the end of the day. Or two. Beans and rice are a dollar a bag. I can throw a pint of whiskey in the mix for four bucks.

"It's the path of least resistance. I keep to myself and spin gossamer magic on the computer. That's about it."

"It must drive you nuts.

"Here you are with your Ivy League education, your writing credentials, interviewed famous people all over the world--Hell! seen more than half the world--and you're no better off than me. Maybe worse off."

"Now who's playing the priest?"

"Doesn't it bother you, wasting your talents?"

"I'm not wasting a thing. I still have the magazine."

"The magazine you claim isn't being read."

"I tend to exaggerate. We have about a hundred thousand readers worldwide. I just wish we had a million domestic and half a million abroad. Then I could make money at it and just be a writer and editor as I lurch toward my dotage. And people in Hell want ice water. I've got about as much of a chance of realizing my wish as they do."

"Cynical fuck."

"Don't start that again. I'm supposed to be 'Asshole,' remember? Ready for dinner?"

"I was wondering about that."

"The corner store is still open. It's your turn to buy the beer."

LIZARD LICK, 9 September, 2005

Even as I type this, I receive a call from Scott Salin, who stayed in Louisiana through the Katrina mess. He is calling from Molly's at the Market, on Decatur Street in the French Quarter. He wants to offer me a chance to get an interview from a man who rode the storm out in New Orleans along with his wife. The gentlemen tells me that a local police official dropped into Molly's--which is crowded right now, 1 p.m. Central Daylight Time in New Orleans, to overflowing. The New Orleans Way. The policeman told the assembled revelers that there was a crime-free night last night in New Orleans--the first time in the city's history something like this might have happened. There are almost no people there anymore. The gentleman I hope to interview, Ty Watford, is off to take friends to a local tattoo artist who has set up a sterile room in one of the French Quarter hotels. Ty and his wife got their tattoos yesterday. The tattoo that they are sporting, and that seems to be catching on, is of the swirling hurricane symbol normally used by The Weather Channel on television, with a large letter "K" in its center. I laugh. That is such a New Orleans thing to do--if you don't mind violating the integrity of your flesh.

Ty and his wife, who are of an artist bent, manufactured a large sign which they have hung on the statue of Jesus behind the St. Louis Cathedral. It says: "Jesus Swept." It is their way of encouraging the people who still remain in New Orleans, in defiance of Mayor Nagin's order that everyone leave until the recovery and clean-up are complete, to get back to work reclaiming their city, he told me.

According the people on the ground in New Orleans the weekend of 9 September, 2005, the French Quarter went basically unscathed after Hurricane Katrina, so that means the heart of darkness of our city is still intact. Bon Temps Roulez.

If you've got the French Quarter, especially from the perspective of people who didn't live in New Orleans, from the perspective of people who felt the only purpose of our city was to be a national adult theme park instead of the hub of all the commerce from the heartland that flowed down the Mississippi River, what else do you need?

I'll tell you. What else you need is the fifth largest commercial port on planet Earth. The true value of New Orleans and that whole southern Louisiana area is the gem in the crown of President Jefferson's Louisiana Purchase. Ships are the most cost-effective way for the United States to move manufactured goods domestically and internationally, and the best way of getting raw materials back into the nation. People like Jeff Jarvis at BuzzMachine.com and others made me so angry because they failed to make the deep analysis that explains why America needs that "Haiti," that "Babylon" that was a city I loved. They failed to understand the history of this nation and why Jefferson was so visionary.

All that water around New Orleans is a Godsend for this country.

The port of New Orleans put Louisiana right up there with Rotterdam and Marseilles.

In an article for the Strategic Forecasting Geopolitical Intelligence Report (http://www.stratfor.com) published on 1 September, 2005, ("New Orleans: A Geopolitical Prize") George Friedman had this to say:

If the Mississippi River was shut to traffic, then the foundations of the economy would be shattered. The industrial minerals needed in the factories wouldn't come in, and the agricultural wealth wouldn't flow out. Alternative routes really weren't available. The Germans knew it too: A U-boat campaign occurred near the mouth of the Mississippi during World War II. Both the Germans and Stratfor have stood with Andy Jackson: New Orleans was the prize.

The Ports of South Louisiana and New Orleans, which run north and south of the city, are as important today as at any point during the history of the republic. On its own merit, POSL is the largest port in the United States by tonnage and the fifth-largest in the world. It exports more than 52 million tons a year, of which more than half are agricultural products -- corn, soybeans and so on. A large proportion of U.S. agriculture flows out of the port. Almost as much cargo, nearly 17 million tons, comes in through the port -- including not only crude oil, but chemicals and fertilizers, coal, concrete and so on.

A simple way to think about the New Orleans port complex is that it is where the bulk commodities of agriculture go out to the world and the bulk commodities of industrialism come in. The commodity chain of the global food industry starts here, as does that of American industrialism. If these facilities are gone, more than the price of goods shifts: The very physical structure of the global economy would have to be reshaped. Consider the impact to the U.S. auto industry if steel doesn't
come up the river, or the effect on global food supplies if U.S. corn and soybeans don't get to the markets.

The problem is that there are no good shipping alternatives. River transport is
cheap, and most of the commodities we are discussing have low value-to-weight ratios. The U.S. transport system was built on the assumption that these commodities would travel to and from New Orleans by barge, where they would be loaded on ships or offloaded. Apart from port capacity elsewhere in the United States, there aren't enough trucks or rail cars to handle the long-distance hauling of these enormous quantities -- assuming for the moment that the economics could be managed, which they can't be.

The focus in the media has been on the oil industry in Louisiana and Mississippi. This is not a trivial question, but in a certain sense, it is dwarfed by the shipping issue. First, Louisiana is the source of about 15 percent of U.S.-produced petroleum, much of it from the Gulf. The local refineries are critical to American infrastructure. Were all of these facilities to be lost, the effect on the price of oil worldwide would be extraordinarily painful. If the river itself became unnavigable or if the ports are no longer functioning, however, the impact to the wider economy would be significantly more severe. In a sense, there is more flexibility in oil than in the physical transport of these other commodities.

And this is how he concluded the article:

New Orleans is not optional for the United States' commercial infrastructure. It is a terrible place for a city to be located, but exactly the place where a city must exist. With that as a given, a city will return there because the alternatives are too devastating. The harvest is coming, and that means that the port will have to be opened soon. As in Iraq, premiums will be paid to people prepared to endure the hardships of working in New Orleans. But in the end, the city will return because it has to.

Geopolitics is the stuff of permanent geographical realities and the way they interact with political life. Geopolitics created New Orleans. Geopolitics caused American presidents to obsess over its safety. And geopolitics will force the city's resurrection, even if it is in the worst imaginable place.

Geography cannot be denied.

All of the great empires of the world have depended upon and been built around rivers: The Tigris and Euphrates that our history books call "the cradle of civilization"; the Nile; the Amazon; the Danube; the Thames; the Yangtze; the Ganges; the Congo; the Mississippi. Thomas Jefferson understood that, as did Mark Twain.

I take some solace, even having lost the New Orleans I knew, in knowing that there will always be a New Orleans because the great river of this country is still there.

What remains to be seen is what the renascent New Orleans will be like. Will they --strike that! I should say, will we--simply throw up highrises to support and feed that corrupt adult theme park that is the architecturally historic French Quarter, besotted on bars and strip clubs and other clip joints, and leave the poor who aren't needed to change the bedclothes and clean the toilets in the hotels to fend for themselves in cities they neither know or love? Or will we, for once, demonstrate a national conscience?

Is it possible, this time, that America can renew its social contract, remember the true context of the promise of democracy, and come up with policies that actually benefit its people?

That's the open question that the lost city of New Orleans has raised for this country, this empire. I'm writing for and to those who think we can provide the right answer for our descendants.

ORLEANS PARISH PRISON (O.P.P.)

LIZARD LICK, 11 September, 2005

There is one other industry that brings income to New Orleans besides tourism and the Port and it is one that was booming before New Orleans was lost: The prison industry.

In 1973, when Sheriff Charles C. Foti, Jr. was first elected to office, the inmate population was less than 800. Today, the total number of municipal, state, and federal inmates is over 6500. This situation is in part due to the increase in the number of inmates who are being held for the State Department of Public Safety and Corrections. The Orleans Parish Criminal Sheriff's Office is now one of the largest jails in the country. - (From the online history of the Orleans Parish Criminal Sheriff's Office, 2003.)

As I wrote in 2003:

Like most news stories, the operative phrase for this one on New Orleans jails is "Follow the money." The Sheriff's Department of Orleans Parish, as every inmate can tell you, makes its income from keeping people incarcerated. Sheriff Foti's office is paid per head by day for every inmate. Incarceration is a growth industry because the voters have been convinced that locking people up makes them safer. Meanwhile, the crime rate in New Orleans and over the state of Louisiana continues to go UP, not down...

... O.P.P. is a vast complex at the heart of the city of New Orleans that houses tens of thousands of locals and tourists. The concrete structures that comprise it are jam-packed every day of the week.

It has been known as a common practice at the Parish Prison to hold inmates who have bonded out until after midnight in order, it's alleged, to bill out charges for another official "day" of incarceration. Because public transportation in New Orleans is either scant or non-existent at whatever later hour after midnight these prisoners were released, many found it difficult to get transport—particularly to far corners of the city like the Lower Ninth Ward and New Orleans East.

Prisoners who could not make bond because of economic hardship were alleged to have been held in this jail for up to six months as they awaited trial. And even tourists were warned not to get themselves arrested during Mardi Gras season because judges, attorneys and other members of the criminal justice system—other than police and Sheriffs—are notoriously unavailable during that time of year. Bonding out is more difficult. Many officials of the court are themselves members of the Mardi Gras krewes, ride on the famous floats or attending balls, and are simply unavailable during that time. More revenue accrues to the Criminal Sheriff's Department during that season by default.

Medical conditions in O.P.P. have always been cited as substandard. Louisiana ACLU reported in a press release dated June 11, 1999:

Dr. John Herbert Niles, M.D.F.A.C.O.G., an expert for the National Prison Project (NPP), has found substandard and life threatening OB/GYN and prenatal care provided to female inmates at Orleans Parish Prison (OPP). His report dated June 2, 1999 confirms conditions documented by attorneys of the NPP, who interviewed over 100 female prisoners at OPP in 1998. Dr. Niles came to New Orleans for two days to review the medical records and speak with 38 inmates as chosen and provided by staff working for Sheriff Charles Foti.

Dr. Niles focused his report on an evaluation of the level of care in the categories of: a) prenatal care; b) postpartum care (following delivery or loss of a pregnancy); c) acute and chronic OB/GYN conditions; and d) preventative and routine OB/GYN care. Using those factors as a baseline, Dr. Niles in his executive summary found, among others:

 * Pelvic exams were not performed at the History and Physical exam or during the course of pregnancy, which would be analogous to going to a dentist without opening your mouth.
 * Pregnant HIV positive patients did not receive proper referrals to the infectious disease clinic at Charity for evaluation and recommendations to protect the fetuses from vertical transmission of the HIV virus.

* Patients at risk for cancer of the cervix and breast cancer did not receive preventive screening with pap smears and mammograms.

* No fetal heart rate monitoring with a doptone occurred during exams of pregnant patients. The in-house clinic personnel monitored fetal well-being by the presence or absence of fetal movement, which ranks as grossly inadequate.

* Preventive prenatal lab tests did not happen at all or in a timely manner as required for: a) spina bifida in the first semester to rule out Down's Syndrome; b) gestational diabetes in the second trimester; c) cultures in the third semester to rule out beta hemolytic strep conditions which could endanger the fetus at the time of delivery

* None of the OB patients had a record of glucose screening during pregnancy at the appropriate time (28 weeks). One had a test at 35 weeks.

* None of the OB patients had prenatal care beginning in the first trimester.

* Despite a policies and procedures manual of the Sheriff's Office mandating prenatal care through Charity's Outpatient Clinic, many patients received few or no such visits to Charity Hospital.

* Overall, the 38 inmate charts reviewed showed substandard care due to: a) inappropriate and inadequate exams; b) failure to perform appropriate lab testing; c) failure to obtain ultrasound exams when indicated; and d) empirical management of sexually transmitted diseases (STD) and vaginal infections
without a definitive diagnosis confirmed by culture or wet mount laboratory evaluation.

* Numerous examples of triple therapies and single dose therapy for "yeast infections" appeared in female patients with Class C medications which could have teratogenic impact (causing genetic abnormalities) on patients in the first trimester and during their pregnancies.

* OPP personnel fail to return patients to Charity for after care following surgery or delivery.

* In an inmate population with a normally high substance abuse and STD percentage, HIV screening was not offered for prenatal patients as called for in standards set by the American College of OB/GYN.

* The monitoring record in the charts for 1998 had produced incomplete and useless information for weekly monitoring of pregnancy status. In 1999, the charts began to show the start of such a

record.

With this being how pregnant women were treated, one can only draw the inference about the treatment of men.

Diabetics, particularly, and heart patients were known to have died because of substandard medical care at O.P.P. facilities.

While a good number of the officers of the New Orleans Police Department were white and resided in other Parishes, Orleans Parish Sheriff Deputies were predominantly young and black. As I learned while attempting to organize the Deputies into a union, turnover among these officers was extremely high. "Turnover here is as bad as McDonald's," one young Deputy told me. "That's because we make about the same money."

Though many carried weapons, and their job was to guard and transport not only local but also state and federal prisoners for one of the largest jails in the United States, the average pay was less than $6.80 per hour. Deputies were required to work twelve hour shifts and donate a certain amount of their time to public service. Many of them complained to me that while the police department employees working Mardi Gras, for example, got overtime pay, Sheriff's Deputies did not. It was counted as part of their public service.

In a Department where charges of cronyism and favoritism were rife, many Deputies also alleged that the "cake" jobs from which additional and premium pay could be garnered--guarding Winn-Dixie supermarkets and that kind of detail--traditionally only went to certain, favored Deputies.

Among the other complaints I heard from Sheriff's Deputies were:

Constant exhaustion from the long hours.
Unsafe working conditions, with tiers and cellblocks meant to house a hundred people often holding as high as three times that many.
Substandard and unsafe furniture in many of the facilities.

Favoritism in assignments and promotions. It was alleged by Deputies

I spoke with, for example that plum assignments like working the
warehouse were often given to relatives of senior officers with little or
no experience and without regard to seniority.

The complaint I heard the most, of course, was about the pay.

As noted, since the 1970s Orleans Parish Prison had become one of the
chief facilities used in the State of Louisiana. There was lots of money
to be made.

The newly elected Sheriff, Marlin Guzman, promised to be open to
reform and an improvement in working conditions.

You wouldn't have learned from brochures offered by the Visitor's and
Convention Bureau that one of the largest jails in the country was right
in the heart of New Orleans, but we locals knew it, and we knew that
business was booming daily at the local court building, hard on the
Orleans Parish Prison complex. As one inmate told me about the
criminal justice system in Southern Louisiana, "Look around you; it's
'just us.'"

The nationally notorious Angola Prison was just a ferry ride away in
Algiers. Besides being known for its rodeo, Angola was known as one
of the worst, most oppressive prisons in the nation. They really do still
pick cotton there.

We now know that rumors circulated about an uprising and hostage-
taking at Orleans Parish Prison during the hurricane were patently
false, another bullet dodged by the lost city.

We' also know now that a skeleton crew of loyal Sheriff's Deputies
rode out Kattina, without food or water for themselves, let alone the
inmates. Prisoners were moved from O.P.P. to facilities throughout the
state and the country ,and some escapes occurred. We now know that
the Greyhound/AmTrak terminal in the Central Business District in
New Orleans became a facility to hold prisoners.

As this is written, there is no official reporting on where the eight
thousand plus prisoners held at one of America's largest prisons

actually are.

REFUGEES IN AMERICA

LIZARD LICK, 13 September, 2005

Two weeks after Hurricane Katrina slammed the Gulf Coast of the United States and flood wall and levees gave way to make the city of New Orleans little more than a watery grave, one million are refugees in America. One million people from Orleans Parish proper and the neighboring communities of Slidell, Gretna, Metairie, Kenner, and Harrahan that together make up the Greater New Orleans metropolitan area, are now spread across the United States from North Carolina, Florida, Tennessee, and Georgia all the way out to California. Though the focus is on those who were evacuated late to shelter in Texas or higher ground in Louisiana, every state--except those also hit, like Mississippi and Alabama--has taken in a few people who only two weeks ago called New Orleans home. And most of these former New Orleanians are going through a kind of culture shock.

Prominent in the lore of New Orleans was that once you'd lived in the Crescent City for a year, you'd discover if you ever tried to leave it that New Orleans had ruined you for life anywhere else.

I can attest that there is some truth to that myth. Though we would proclaim for years that living in New Orleans was distinctly not like living in America--socially, politically or economically--it seems that only now is that message beginning to be taken seriously.

In many parts of New Orleans, even the structures in which we lived were un-American in their facilities, layout and architecture. If you lived in the "historic" parts of New Orleans, like the French Quarter, Marigny, Bywater or the Lower Nine, it was likely you lived in half of a double shotgun, for example.

Unlike trailer or prefab homes in other rural parts of America that are designed along the wide layout that you might find in most houses, shotguns--so-called because it was said you could shoot off a shotgun at the front door of the house and have the buckshot go unimpeded straight out the back door--are built long. Most have pocket doors, usually left open, separating the first two rooms, with the bedchambers and kitchens toward the back of the house. Bathrooms are usually boxed in somewhere between the bedchambers or at the very back of the long stretch of house, embedded into one side of the inner hallway-like walls. There are traditionally no chambers on the "inside"/ separating wall between the two halves of the double shotgun. All the usable living space is laid out toward the outer walls. This design was done to maximize airflow through the dwelling during sweltering New Orleans summers. But it is hell on any sense of personal privacy. If you lived in a half a double shotgun, it was very likely that you had to walk through someone else's bedroom to get to the wash room and toilet.

If you lived in the above-mentioned historic districts of the city, it was also extremely likely that your residence was made of wood. There are few stone structures in those parts of town outside of the French Quarter unless they were built in the latter part of the twentieth century. It's also likely that your sewer connected to terracotta French drainage systems that originated hundreds of years ago. In businesses throughout the French Quarter you could see warning signs about what you should and should not put in the toilets and the best procedure for flushing them. The drainage off the side of your house most likely fed into a brickwork trench that sloped toward the street with holes at intervals to begin taking some of the water off into the sewer system below.

On many streets, your sidewalk, too, would be worn and irregular brickwork, often with up-croppings that were like virtual cliffs in the path, from where the old live oaks had spread the roots and begun winning the battle between man and nature. These streets gave you the gait of a drunk even when you weren't loaded.

Even the language was different in New Orleans. We used words not found in other parts of Louisiana, let alone the rest of the United States. "Yat?" ("Where you at?" Our equivalent of, "How are you doing?") "Yerm?" (Ya' hear me? Meaning, "Do you understand what I mean or what I'm saying?") And so on.

Rather than the traditional American practice of bars having a "Last

Call," there are bars in New Orleans that haven't closed in years. Jim Monaghan, Jr., a friend of mine who owns Molly at the Market on Decatur Street, bragged to a New York Times reporter this past weekend that "This place has been closed for 29 hours in the last 31 years." (Molly's was never open 24 and 7, though. Checkpoint Charlie's at Decatur and Esplanade Ave, right down the street, had not closed its doors, for even an hour, prior to Katrina. The running joke about that place was that when cops tried to get the owner, Igor, to close it during Hurricane Betsy a few years ago, he I had told them he no longer had "any idea where the damned keys are.")

And, as FEMA officials have quickly discovered, it was common not to have a checking account in New Orleans. The "underground economy" thrived in that destitute city. It was as common as not to get your pay in cash in New Orleans—even at so-called "respectable" establishments. I personally know that a person can live in New Orleans for years without ever drawing a paycheck, thus never being on the books of their employers. "Cash and carry" was a meaningful and operative phrase in New Orleans. If you worked in the construction industry in this city of widespread renovations, or in many parts of the service industry in this city of thousands of bars and restaurants, it was not uncommon to get all of your compensation in cash.

This was not America.

And this is just the tip of the cultural iceberg that is being faced by New Orleanian refugees, many of them out of their city for the first time, as they are placed in the real America.

ASIDE: In this country where quibbles over terminology are so damned important, it has been reported in the Mouthpiece Media that some people object to the use of the term "refugee" to refer to the former citizens of New Orleans. You got people with little more than the clothes on their backs, no jobs, often no homes and no money to speak of showing up in your town seeking refuge, what else would you call them? That's what we'd call them if they were in Kosovo or Iraq, isn't it? Enough.

The people who actually lived in New Orleans knew two things: The businesses that fueled New Orleans were primarily owned by people who--even though they might be descended from families that once lived in New Orleans--now lived outside of Orleans Parish for the most part. The money, the amenities, the culture that you might see in the rest of America was out in Kenner, Metairie, Slidell, Chalmette, etc. So were the traditional suburban tract homes, the large estates, the strip malls, and discount outlets. (I knew at least one person who spent months looking for bed sheets because he lived in the French Quarter and buying any at reasonable prices meant getting out to the 'burbs and he didn't own a vehicle.) The people who actually lived within Orleans Parish were predominantly poor, predominantly black, and mostly worked for these old families of business owners who had abandoned the city long ago and now fed off of its attraction for tourists from the outside.

The exceptions to this rule where those few very wealthy people who lived on and around St. Charles Avenue, traditionalists inured to many of the problems of the rest of Orleans Parish, even the crime--because they could keep police patrols thick in their neighborhoods--and those out around the Lakeview area, far from the maddening crowd. These latter two groups joined the rest of the residents in disdaining the rest of America and the people outside the Parish as not really being New Orleanians and therefore déclassé.

Particularly looked down upon by most New Orleanians were the people of Chalmette, who were openly referred to as "Chalmatians" because, unlike those who flocked to Kenner, Metairie, etc., many were poor white trash. They fit the picture of America that was dubbed "trailer trash" during the 1990s in the traditional New Orleans stereotype.

The second thing we all knew in New Orleans was that despite the long history of black residency in the city, the cultural contributions of blacks to literature, food, and especially the music notoriety and tradition of New Orleans, blacks were always second class citizens in the hierarchy and political priorities of the Crescent City. Blacks were also the poorest of the poor and relegated to the most neglected neighborhoods in the Parish. We knew that there was a genteel but de facto economic plantation system that still abided and was severely enforced in New Orleans, that whites often chose to describe as part of New Orleans' "charm." It wasn't charming if you were black and one of its victims, though.

Here's one example: If you were in any of the drinking establishments in the French Quarter and environs, which numbered over 200 in the Quarter alone in 2001, about a month before one annual event that happens during the Season, you'd begin to hear the (predominantly white—we'll get to that below) bartenders start to complain. The event? The traditional Bayou Classic football game between Grambling and Southern Universities. The event, officially known as the State Farm Bayou Classic, began in 1974 and has always been held in New Orleans. It was originally held at Tulane Stadium but as it began drawing visitors from around the country it was moved to the Superdome.

Please note: according to official figures, the Bayou Classic pumps an average of $30 million a year into the New Orleans economy.

If you ask any of these bartenders why they so dread the Bayou Classic, their responses range from subtle to overt. "Blacks just don't tip." (A lie.) "They drive out my regular customers." (Is that because the bar is busier and there's no place to sit? Is that because you believe your regular customers don't want to be around these tourists?) "Those people just don't know how to act! They are rude and obnoxious." (In my experience they are no more rude, obnoxious or unruly than frat boys from other places that I've served "Huge Ass" beers to on Bourbon Street and elsewhere.) Besides, for my money, the crowd that takes over Bourbon Street and other downtown environs during the Bayou Classic often tends to dress better.

The reader will recall that I mentioned how bartenders were considered the top of the service industry food chain in New Orleans. New Orleans being a city whose population was over sixty percent black, you might assume that mixology would provide an avenue for economic opportunity for a black person—and you'd be wrong.

I'm black and I was a bartender in New Orleans, in and around the

French Quarter. I was an exception to the rule, and astute people, including some of my fellow bartender friends, commented on that fact. By a rough estimate, if you took the lower French Quarter, say from St. Louis Street to Esplanade Avenue, the Mississippi to that notorious dividing line at St. Claude Avenue; then you added on the Marigny and Bywater---same boundaries of River and St. Claude, lower boundary of Poland Avenue, where you reached the Industrial Canal; there were approximately 300 bars, give or take 50. At the time I was bartending in New Orleans (2002 – 2004) at various establishments, you could count all the Black bartenders in that quadrant of New Orleans, a prime zone, and not exhaust the fingers on two hands. That rough estimate tells you that only slightly over three percent of the bartenders--when we don't count the large hotels on Canal Street--in the Quarter proper, Marigny and Bywater, were black. When you take that estimate into consideration, it becomes understandable why the Bayou Classic got bad mouthed.

WALKING WHILE BLACK

In the interest of full disclosure, I must point out to the reader that I particularly sensitive to this issue of race and class in New Orleans because I consider myself a victim of it. A Google search on my name will not only bring up my past writing on technology issues of Andover.net (now OSTG,) citations from my magazine, G21.net, and other publications, but also--and prominently--a 2003 story in the New Orleans alternative weekly, The Gambit, where I I was featured on the paper's cover.

That story prompted letters from friends all over the United States including my editor on this book. If I had not been something of a well-known face in and around the French Quarter before the newspaper story, I was afterward. For months, there were few places I could go in most of New Orleans where complete strangers, having seen my picture on the cover of the Gambit and read the story would not walk up to me and proclaim, "Hey, ain't you the guy who got fucked over by the cops?"

The subject of the story was my arrest and incarceration on Esplanade Avenue, in front the Circle K convenience store, which many readers may have seen in television reports about the French Quarter.

My crimes? Well, I think I proved in court, and the local newspaper concurred: 1) Walking While Black, and, 2) Having a young white roommate.

The Reader's Digest version of the story is that my roommate and I decided to attend a party together on Dauphine Street, the next block over from our apartment, after he got off work one evening. We decided that it would be a good idea to bring over some beer. He gave me $7 to purchase the beer in the Circle K while he stood outside smoking a cigarette. The clerk in the store said, for reasons I still don't fully fathom, that she couldn't unlock the beer cooler. I came back out and explained the situation and handed my roomie his money back.

A New Orleans police car had pulled up to the corner while I was inside the store and immediately called me over. The asked what I had handed the man, and I told them—truthfully--$7. They asked why I had done that and I explained about the party and the beer.

From there my nightmare began. It's all documented in court papers, the Gambit Weekly story, and at my own G21.net. I ended up spending almost two weeks in jail and about $3000 in legal fees. (Most of the money for the legal fees was raised in benefits and donations from my friends who were in the bartender, stripper, bike delivery, and gay communities in the French Quarter and Marigny, though other people around the country also helped.)

The most troubling part of the entire experience was listening to one of the two white police officers blatantly lie on the stand in court. Luckily, my lawyer was able to expose his lies, the judge looked exasperated, and the Assistant District Attorney who had been assigned to my case came up to me and apologized, before everyone present, for all I had been made to endure.

Everyone who has examined the details of what happened--attorneys, judges, friends---reached the same conclusion: What happened to me could happen to any black man walking the streets of New Orleans.

Coincidentally, my arrest happened during a time when Councilwoman Jackie Clarkson was pressuring the police to "clean up" the French Quarter, increase arrest rates, and was trying to pass ordinances that would have dire consequences for service workers who worked late shifts in the French Quarter, like black kitchen staff, street artists, and performers in Jackson Square.

Coincidentally, neither of the two cops who arrested and charged me lived in Orleans Parish. My ordeal went on longer than it should have, and cost additional legal fees, because it was like pulling teeth to get even one of the two police officers to come to New Orleans and show up in court when they were not on duty.

It wouldn't surprise me if these two were among the 500 cops, one third of the New Orleans Police Department, who reportedly went AWOL after Katrina.

DOWN AND OUT, WITH DEATH ALL AROUND

As I often attempted to document in my magazine, published from New Orleans (and mostly from the Ninth Ward) for four years, when you were looking at New Orleans there is no way, I say no way, that you were looking at America.

I was not the only one writing and saying this. Others were, too. That is why it is particularly maddening today to hear the chorus of surprise about the conditions in the Ninth Ward of New Orleans. It was a Big Story in the September 19 editionof Newsweek magazine (that hit news stands on12 September).

I just have to ask myself, as I'm sure other people from New Orleans, the Ninth Ward, and especially black people must ask: "Where was Newsweek in 2001, or 1991, or all the rest of the time this has been going on for and to us?"

Our being poor, so poor that one out of three of us couldn't afford a car, making around $10,000, living on devastated streets and being treated like dirt in our own city wasn't new. This is what daily life was like here for a long time. Why did it take a hurricane for you to go beyond the French Quarter and see the real New Orleans?

A lot of us can't help but suspect that you're scared you'll have to put up with us in your cities now. We have been evacuated to places near you. And, like those folks up in Baton Rouge who lined up at the gun stores so that they could "deal with all the 'Yats," you are a little afraid, aren't you?

I do hear a few voices speaking about some redress of the circumstances that led to the crushing poverty in the "American Haiti" called New Orleans. But they are very few. Let the Saints keep on losing...

NEW ORLEANS, 21 January, 2005: It's been an interesting few days. Since I'm urban camping, there's been no telephone access, no Internet access, and no food. Here's the thing about people in New Orleans: Just about everyone will buy you a beer, but it's like pulling hen's teeth to get a sandwich. So I've been living on beer and water for the last few days, other than a slice a pizza from Nick.

Matt comes over and is always ready for a beer, so he buys me a couple, too. He is the bearer of more bad news: a check for work I did for a company called Brainfuse has not arrived.

When I awakened this morning, the Lord put it in my mind that I hadn't touched base with Scott--probably the only other person up and alert at this time in the a.m. besides Yours Unruly--and that he'd certainly help. Ten bucks right now could make a huge difference until the Brainfuse check arrives.

I telephoned him with my last quarter (one of the "luxuries" of living in the 'hood is that pay phones are, of necessity, cheaper than most places) and we shall rendezvous later this morning. El hamdur'Allah.

NEW ORLEANS, 16 February, 2005

The half double shotgun where I have been urban camping has is being worked on again today. Nick and his uncle have left the other renovation they were working on and promise to now pay full attention to my space. I should, thus, have a stove by the weekend. Maybe even a shower. I can dream.

Meanwhile, the new pay period begins at ACORN today, so that I have the chance of finally making salary. Who knows, perhaps someone will also remember that I was told I was hired to work on the lead-abatement project. People around me are beginning to take decisions and make actions that shall directly impact my life. I have turned on the auto-pilot and decided to let the plane do what it does best.

The latest edition of G21.net went in the bag yesterday, two days earlier than scheduled, to my great relief, but cost me every bit of money I had until payday, which is a week away. So I am scratching around for ways to come up with other money in my "spare" time.

Wish me luck!

NEW ORLEANS, 19 February, 2005

THINGS HAVE CHANGED DRASTICALLY in every area of my life
EXCEPT cash-flow. (Of course.)

First the personal: As of today I have a stove! Yay! Now all I need is
some food to cook on it and something to cook that food in... Ehm...
But that's a drastic improvement. I have a shower, too! Double yay!
And a bathroom cabinet with a mirror in which to shave instead of
using the back of a CD, as I have for about a month now. No furniture
yet, but the place is still kind of a construction site. There's still paper
from the painting on a couple of the floors, there's still another window
to be hung, and most of the doors are still not installed. But it is
starting to look like an apartment.

On the professional front, like a bolt out of the blue, I have suddenly
been moved to working among the senior staff at ACORN. I have two
new projects on my plate, as of yesterday, that will move me away
from simply being a door-knocker. The subject of my facility with
reports and budgets was broached. There are new learning and/or
training sessions on this week's agenda. I have a meeting at the
Mayor's office this week, too.

The one subject that was not broached was money. (Of course.) Things
were coming at me so hard and fast yesterday that it was all I could do
to keep up. I needed to absorb the information I was being hit with,
immediately embark on a new project, and try to assess this sudden
change in the lay of the land.

I'm going to take my supervisor--with whom I'll be working on a
radically different basis soon, it seems--aside and ask him about the
money thang this morning.

POLAND STREET, NEW ORLEANS, 20 February, 2005

My friend and landlord, Nick, loaned me twenty-five bucks so that I
might eat yesterday. He and his uncle joked about when I would first

use my new stove and we decided that it should be yesterday, which had been a frustrating day for us all. Rather than work on this apartment, they had spent the day working on the toilet of Nick's tenants next door. It seems that the plumber who was supposed to have come to fix it, a New Orleanian, first called to say that he had a flat tire and later that his truck had some other unknown problem. So the job was left to Nick and Drew.

Nick said, "Doesn't it seem like people in this town are just weird? They don't behave like people anywhere else. There is something seriously wrong about them."

My supposed ride to work, a rarity in that I usually walk the forty-minute journey there and so was glad of the offer, never materialized. When I realized that she wasn't going to show on time, I called in and then started my trek. When I arrived, it was to discover that instead of going out door-knocking we were to take part in a caravan promoting a candidate in district 96. The effort of putting together the caravan squandered the entire day, New Orleans style, and even took me into overtime on top of my overtime. I arrived home angry and miffed. I said, "All I could think about today was that the one thing you can depend on from someone from New Orleans is that you can't depend on them."

Drew, who is about my age or perhaps even older, had just gone through a breakup with his latest inamorata. She just has a problem with forming a relationship, he observed. He had invited her to dinner and she had demurred. He told her, he said, "I understand what you're doing. If you go back into your shell, you'll probably stay there for the rest of your life." He told Nick and me that she responded, "Yes, you are right. That is probably true." Then he gave us a look of bewilderment.

Drew said, "I don't know what it is about these people in New Orleans! Is it the effects of their strange Catholicism? Is that there are too many Irish? I can't figure it out."

I didn't say anything, having noted that Drew seems to have a thing about Irish Catholics. I could have said that most of the heritage here is actually French Catholic. I could have said, as I heard someone observe in a tavern one night, that New Orleanians didn't learn from the Romans about how too much lead--in the old paint dust from the constantly renovated houses and in the water--constantly ingested into your system will eventually drive you mad. I could have said that this subterranean system of excess and sex and living with the dead above ground amongst you leads to a certain quirky instability. I could have said that it is as infectious as malaria and has many of the same effects. But I didn't....

Nick's $25 went quickly because in order to cook, I had to buy pots, utensils, a bowl, and food. When I threw in bath soap, a pack of cigarettes, and beer on top of that, I was left with less than three dollars. It is still three days before payday at my All-Day Job.

What food did I buy?

Red beans and rice, of course! What else can I afford?

After my morning shower (yay!) today, I had a golden moment. I felt three things that I have not felt since living here on Poland Street: Clean, warm and comfortable. It was an epiphany, of sorts. I felt good, like I'm not just urban camping any longer, but actually have an apartment. Do you think that has anything to do with being able to cook at home again?

My pals Matt Stowell and Steve Hessey came to the rescue on this day off. Matt gave me a small cash infusion to keep me in a good mental state until payday, we went out for drinks--where we met Steve -- and he tossed me a pack of unfiltered GPCs. (We jokingly call them "Ghetto Pal Cigarettes" because they are obviously concocted from the floor-leavings of some tobacco plant and sold to us brothers for a song.)

When I asked Steve for a recommendation for a good place to pick up a cooking knife, he volunteered to give me a cleaver he had been "experimenting" on to turn into a fish-shaped implement. I was chuffed. When we met him at the Sugar Park Tavern--another place around the way from my place (did I just say that?) here near the

Industrial Canal separating the rest of the New Orleans from the Lower Nine, I asked for a recommendation for good meat to add to the beans I was cooking when Matt popped over.

Steve gave me a book, entitled Cleese Encounters, about Monty Python veteran John Cleese, in which to conceal the cleaver. "The last thing you want to do is walk down the streets of the Ninth Ward carrying a meat cleaver in your hand, my friend," he joked. "I can just hear the cops callin' you in now."

Instead of a recommendation for purchasing the meat for my dinner, Steve gave me a Robert's (pronounced "row-bear's," in Nawlins) bag with a couple of steaks in it. Yes, indeed.

If you're a poor man in New Orleans and you have friends, you have a hook-up.

Matt got on my case, on the walk back to my house, about going hungry this week. "Why didn't you call me, man?" he said. "You know I wouldn't let you go hungry. You only have a couple of days left until your payday. When are you gonnah learn to swallow some of that pride of yours?"

I had to acknowledge that he had a good point.

The challenge I face right now is finding balance.

My new Day Job demands a great deal of my time and energy, as does my magazine. That leaves little time or energy for a social life: Something required by all the energy demanded by the former two in order to recharge young Rod's batteries.

I also have some political goals, if I am to stay here in Nawlins. This system and this mentality MUST change. My Day Job accommodates that desire.

The social issue is more problematic, both because of my own hermetic tendencies and my lack of free time. A girlfriend would motivate me toward being more inclined toward having a personal life.

So I cleaned my apartment this weekend, as much as I could considering that it still resembles a construction site more than a place where someone actually lives, because I prefer to work in an orderly environment. My "monk's cell" mode. And I attempted to visualize the possibility of sharing this place with another person instead of keeping it all to myself.

When considering these two options, the latter was preferable.

Yes, it would be a large apartment for a single man, by New Orleans standards, and expensive. But privacy matters a great deal to me. I thrive on having time alone in which to complete my work without distractions from outside sources. Silence is something that is a requirement in my days.

A roommate would provide social company but also require compromising the isolation I most need in order to cogitate and write. Because my Day Job and political goals require giving an enormous amount of "face time" every day, I feel that coming home to a quiet, calm and empty environment would be good and provide the kind of mental and spiritual balance I am seeking.

I've been focused on heat, it being winter. But my Real Concern should be, this being New Orleans, that this apartment I am considering making my home has NO AIR CONDITIONING! Yikes!

LIZARD LICK, 13 September, 2005

Living in New Orleans was a kaleidoscopic series of parties, bar room conversations, jazz funerals, festivals and encounters, as befits this most Catholic of cities. The prominence of the Catholic Church, its rituals and even saints co-identified with those of New Orleans' long voodoo tradition, lends itself to an atmosphere of successive festivals and elaborate rituals. These infused the lives of New Orleanians as much as the famous above-ground crypts. So much of our life was about sex and death....

When I lived on Esplanade Avenue, in an apartment immediately above a bar called Checkpoint Charlie's, the story came out that a man who had lived there three years earlier had hung himself in the large French window that overlooked the intersection of Decatur Street and Esplanade Avenue, directly across from the old Mint Building. He didn't just hang himself, though, as the tale was related to me. First he injected himself with Drano, just to make sure. He hung himself in that window so that everybody, all the revelers coming up Decatur Street from nights at Molly's at the Market or The Abbey, say, would see him up there dead on their way to their homes and never forget.

Two days later, I was told that the restaurant where I was working had had its own brush with death. A few years earlier, two ex-employees had herded a group of the remaining employees of the place--about five or six people, the story goes--into the meat cooler, made them get down on their knees, and proceeded to blow their heads off with shotguns.

When I freaked out about this presence of Death all around me, one of the waiters at the place commented: "Oh, lighten up, Rod! There ain't many places you live in Nawlins where somebody didn't either get killed or kill themselves."

I understood why the Ghost Tours did such brisk business. It wasn't hard to find a story about death in this city, even away from the cemeteries.

Somewhere in every story out of New Orleans, there is death or sex or both. The city veritably dripped sex and death, it hung all around you, it oozed out of the pores of the place and welled up from the sewers.

(ALMOST) SEX AND (ALMOST) DEATH IN NAWLINS

NEW ORLEANS, 5 December, 2002

There are women coming and going in my life right now "...speaking of Michelangelo", as the great poet said.

I seem to be stuck in the upper reaches of the alphabet, as far as these women go. I'm trapped between F and L and can't manage to escape. (What ever happened to all the women named Suzy?) There is something to recommend each of them but there is also something that would tell a sane person to run like hell in the other direction. A sane person, not me.

THIS IS MY WEEK OF METAPHORICAL SEEDS & STEMS.

That is, I'm living on ketchup sandwiches and waiting for a Web project I'm working on to be completed so I can send an invoice, waiting for the shifts at the bar to commence again. I have four days off in actuality this week, so I can play catch up. But I also just (barely) made the rent for my new digs, which means I'm so broke I can't even pay attention.

I went to the bar and got an advance on my shift pay for Saturday today, just to buy lots of cold cuts so I can eat between now and then.

The weather even seems to collude against me. When I left my drafty hovel today it looked and felt like the "snow weather" I used to see in New England. New Orleans isn't supposed to be this way. Our houses aren't built for it. It deprives us of sleep, shivering below our thin blankets and hoping our foot-warmer space heaters aren't burning electricity into mega-bills that were meant to be next month's meals.

So, during this time, I try to stay in my Hobbit Hole as long as my limbs will allow, and peck out the code for that Web site I should have delivered, electronically, to California last week when I was scurrying

Figure 11. Carnival masks in a shop window.

around trying to hustle up the rent. I don't even have a chair.

It's tough work sitting on the plywood platform that the last occupant used to put his bed on because the main room here is--well, you know.

It's either that or perched on two cushions Scott gave me, my computer on my lap, for as long as my back can handle it.

I sit there as long as I can, reading the requisite notes and bouncing from program to program to tweak the graphics and make sure all the links work and the spelling is good, yatta-yatta-yatta.

THEN I FEEL LIKE I WANT TO SCREAM!!!

I have to get out of here.

I toss my laptop into her pack and go off looking for somewhere to "jack in", as William Gibson put it in Neuromancer. Somewhere to rejoin my own life where it is warm.

It may be cold in space, but on the Internet we don't feel any temperature at all.

I've been meaning to mention to you that what I perform is called "Three-dot Journalism." Both Charles McCabe and Herb Caen at the San Francisco Comical were quite good at it, though from different perspectives from each other or myself. Jimmy Breslin indulges in it now and again, as well. It's an episodic, old man's way of presenting the life around you.

I think of this because, reading over my previous writing, I came away feeling that I was more episodic than usual.

HERE'S AN EXAMPLE: One of my bosses at The Spotted Cat, the bar I work for, suggested that I might want to attend this Prosperity ceremony that a voodoo priestess is performing there tomorrow (Friday) night. I said I'd consider it. I made an off-handed quip about the fact that another person I knew who'd moved to this city had her parents warn her to stay away from the voodoo thang down here. The parents offered my friend money just to keep her away from it.

But as you'd imagine, being part of any kind of quasi-magical ritual, especially one that claims to be based on a religion, is not exactly a Rod-ly cup of grog. I try to be politic about such things, but it just ain't me. So I quip about a story I've heard (deliver a parable) or I say nada.

After all, you cannot petition the Lord with prayer. Heh!

NEW ORLEANS, 7 December, 2002

Of course I always get trapped by the Muse of Irony when I make statements like that last one. As Fate would have it, I was at The Spotted Cat for the Prosperity ceremony.

I went there to jack in and send off the Web project I had been designing. As it was late in the day, I arrived about an hour and half before the ritual was to commence. People started buying me beers. It was quite a show and so I ended up sitting next to Trish, my boss, when the priestess came around blowing the smoke of Chango [the voodoo patron of Prosperity] through a cigar so that we would become more prosperous.

Haitian music swayed in the background and lots of friends of the priestess showed up to take part in the event. It made for a better day for Greg, the Friday day shift bartender, so somebody got a bit more prosperous, at least. Obviously, if my next journal entry is written from Rio de Janeiro rather than this little hovel in Nawlins, you'll know that Chango's favors work.

I LIKE TREES

This is something most of my closest friends know about me. So even though I whine about my hovel, it has one saving grace: There are windows on three sides of the place and each affords me a wonderful view of trees. There is a willow tree that overhangs the stairs up to my place and festoons my kitchen window. There are oaks, palms and jasmine to the east. Out of every window, I see trees first. Trees obscure the houses across the street to the west; only trees to the south; trees before the pink house to the east. I have no northern window.

Sitting on cushions on the floor as I type, I can pretend that I live in the center of a great forest. I see only the pink head of the jasmine to my right, only the golden autumn leaves of the oaks before me. The sky is grey. Now I am alone.

TALES OF WOMEN

I met "Fashionable," a young Korean writer, a couple of months back. We got together a couple of times. She took me to a poetry reading (something I never do because of my low opinion of most of the participants). I took her to the most recent "Iron Chef" party some of my friends were having. We've gone out to lunch. She comes and sees me at the bar. Most of my friends here think she is too airy and flighty. Part of the suspicion about her has to do, I believe, with the fact that she thinks everything and everyone is invariably "sweet" and "nice." We're a jaundiced crowd in these precincts and don't believe anyone can be that unshakably uncritical.

She came by to see me last Saturday evening when my friend Jak, whose era at the Cat preceded my own, was also visiting. I introduced them and continued my rounds of the imbibers. It was not long before I saw the tanks start moving. I have seen Jak's campaigns on women before. They are as subtle as one might expect from General Patton. Before long Jak and Fashionable were gliding across the dance floor cheek to cheek. I went on with my job. I was only simmering.

Eventually Fashionable left the place. So did Jak. But he came back at the end of my shift, while I was having my shift drink and chatting with Daniel, the night bartender. He came back, he announced, to let me know that he was going to begin dating Fashionable. Thanks a lot, I said. Just thought I should tell you upfront, he said. He left.

Now I was boiling, of course. So I left and made my way to Molly's at the Market for my usual after-shift drink with Lloyd, the back room bartender there. As usual, I was one of Lloyd's first and only customers. Except for this woman. The Dancer, we'll call her. She was cute enough and willing enough to talk.

We left together and began a night of travels and travails (I forgot about my laptop and almost lost it!), dancing, long talks, more dancing. She wanted me to see her house in MidCity, so she drove us out there. We decided that we would go dancing again this weekend. I got her phone number. It was way early. I was down to a slow simmer again. So I went back out.

I was awakened by a neighbor pounding on my door telling me that my boss was looking for me.

CRAP! The bar! We open early on Sundays! I was MIA for the first time ever and figured all was lost.

They had called all my friends, the hospitals, the police, my landlord and the morgue.

"We were worried," Ed told me when I arrived at the Cat. "It's not like you to ever be late, let alone not show up at all." Later he told me that he had heard that I was out with a woman the night before.

"What? From who?"

You can't do anything in the French Quarter without everyone
knowing it. If you want to keep a secret, you have to leave the
reservation, Scott quips.

Then Ed handed me a note. It was from Fashionable. She had come in
earlier, planning to see to me, and had brought me some food. "It's in
the microwave," Ed told me.

Okay.

Luckily, I had not lost my job. In fact, I got a lot of good-natured
ribbing rather than a lecture. I worked out my shift with a wicked
hangover. One more day and the work week would come to an end.

Jak came by on my Monday shift to ask me for Fashionable's address.
When he left, Scott asked me why I hadn't told him to sod off and
withheld the information. "You don't have to help him hurt you!"

Well, I believe it's never us that choose; it's always the women. I
wasn't making any kind of campaign on Fashionable anyway. I don't
make campaigns on women any longer. I wait for them to catch me.

All week, I've been thinking about calling both The Dancer and
Fashionable. I've called neither because I had the Web project to
complete. Now that's behind me, so I may call one or both of them.
But, this morning, I awakened remembering that I had not seen this
muralist who had just moved back to town from New York, in a couple
of weeks. I did her a favor and then she simply disappeared. (I know
what you're thinking already! Be quiet.) I think that it's time she should
drop into the Cat again. I really want to call The Dancer.

LIZARD LICK, 13 September, 2005

New Orleans was to America what Beirut, before the 1970s, had been
for most of the more orthodox countries of the Middle East. We were
America's playground. After Las Vegas, whose total focus was

gambling, New Orleans was the place to go to indulge all of the sins to which the flesh his prone. New Orleans, we locals used to say, was where people come to do the things they'd only dream about doing at home.

We had it all: Sex, booze, drugs, and gambling.

Want to drink all night and walk home (or to the hotel) at sunrise? You could do it in New Orleans. Lots of the bars never closed. There was no such thing as "Last Call" in New Orleans. If the bar you were in did close for the night, you could just walk a couple of blocks to another one that was still open. Let the good times roll!

Looking for hookers? New Orleans has 'em. Want your sex a little more tame? There were the notorious Bourbon Street and environs strip clubs, Temptations, Larry Flynt's Hustler Club, and on and on.

Figure 12. The world-renowned Saturn Bar in the Ninth Ward.

Hey! Are you feeling lucky? The crown jewel of Canal Street--that long border between the French Quarter and CBD--originally built to actually be a canal, was the large beige and neon glittering Harrah's casino. As long as you were gambling, be it anything from poker to slots, the drinks were free. If you got hungry, there were cafes on site.

Just keeping pumping those slot machines, play some poker or blackjack, my friend.

Almost every bar in New Orleans had video poker machines. Those machines made so much for the establishments that you weren't required to buy a drink as long as you pumped more of your hard-earned one, five and ten dollar bills into them. Lots of people's lives revolved around the poker machines because you always ran into someone who had just "hit." Besides, the odds of making a big score on a poker machine were exponentially better than those you could expect from the state lottery.

That was one of the dangers in the bartender lifestyle. You began to believe in the myths about the video poker machines, that you could pay attention to action on those machines and figure when they were due to hit. Some seemed to know, some didn't. Many a New Orleans bartender would tell you how a five dollar bet in poker machine had saved his or her bacon. I even have one those stories myself.

For all of these reasons, these playground reasons, New Orleans was despised by the rest of Louisiana. As A.J. Liebling noted in his wonderful book on the former governor of Louisiana, Earl Long, The Earl of Louisiana, it was an unwritten rule of Louisiana politics that no politician from New Orleans would ever be elected governor of the state. Though it was the largest city in the state, and the source of most of its revenue, New Orleans was the stepchild. Most of the rest of Louisiana was Southern Baptist, and Alexandria and Baton Rouge were considered more representative of the way Louisianians viewed themselves than that sinful, Catholic New Orleans. In a state where corruption was legendary, New Orleans was considered even more corrupt.

It was bad enough that New Orleans was not considered part of America; New Orleans was not even considered part of its own state. We didn't speak the same language. Besides the customs and confession that separated New Orleans from the rest of Louisiana, there were the words, expressions and accent. The New Orleans accent has often been compared to that of the Bronx or Brooklyn, in New York City, as opposed to the characteristic southern drawl. Many

136

people from the Ninth Ward sound more like French than English speakers. And then there is the influence of the long-ago influx of Acadians, now just called Cajuns.

LIZARD LICK, 16 September, 2005

There is a different attitude toward death in New Orleans from that of any other city in America. Where America shuns, denies, and hides from Death, New Orleans celebrates it.

New Orleans was the great funeral city of America. We demonstrated with our famous Jazz Funerals, also known as "Second Lines."

Behind the horse-drawn carriage carrying the body of the deceased, there followed a brass band and then the revelers, the people paying their respects to the one who had passed on, dancing to the music of a traditional brass ensemble. There was plenty of beer and whatever else people wanted to drink, mostly held in plastic "go" cups, in the hands of those who followed the funeral procession as it snaked through the streets of our river city.

Anybody who was anybody in New Orleans had a Second Line at the end of his her funeral. You would be remembered, in most folks estimation, by how many people heard about your Second Line and showed up to be part of your last party.

The late JazzMan Danny Barker, writing in his book Bourbon Street Black noted that the funeral is seen as "a major celebration":

The roots of the Jazz Funeral date back to Africa. Four centuries ago, the Dahomeans of Benin and the Yoruba of Nigeria, West Africa were laying the foundation for one of today's most novel social practices on the North American Continent, the Jazz Funeral.

The secret societies of the Dahomeans and Yoruba people assured fellow tribesmen that a proper burial would be performed at the time of death. To accomplish this guarantee, resources were pooled to form what many have labeled an early form of insurance.

Figure 13. A Jazz Funeral in New Orleans.

When slaves were brought to America, the idea of providing a proper burial to your fellow brother or sister remained strong. As time passed, these very same concepts that were rooted in African ideology became one of the basic principles of the social and pleasure club. The social and pleasure club guaranteed proper burial conditions as did many fraternal orders and lodges to any member who passed. These organizations were precursors to the concept of burial insurance and the debit insurance companies.

The practice of having music during funeral processions, Danny Barker said, was added to the basic African pattern of celebration for most aspects of life including death. As the Brass Band became increasingly popular during the early 18th Century, they were frequently called on to play processional music. Eileen Southern in The Music of Black American wrote, "On the way to the cemetery it was customary to play very slowly and mournfully a dirge, or an 'old Negro spiritual' such as "Nearer My God to Thee," but on the return from the cemetery, the band would strike up a rousing, "When the Saints Go Marching In', or a ragtime song such as "Didn't He Ramble." Sidney Bechet, the renown New Orleans JazzMan after observing the celebrations of the jazz funeral stated, "music here is as much a part of death as it is of life." [All of the preceding is excerpted from The Soul of New Orleans Web site]

It was not unusual, when I lived in the lost city, to hear the quip, "Yeah, you talkin' shit now but you be the first one up there cryin' and dancin' my Second Line, won't ya?"

The New Orleans Way.

NEW ORLEANS - 29 March, 2004

Only an hour or two could have made the difference. According to people who saw the large pool of blood, according to the doctors in the Trauma Unit at Charity Hospital, if I had remained unconscious for another hour it would all have been over. The Emergency Medical Technicians (EMTs) who rush me to the hospital gave me the designation "Unknown Mackerel" because I had no identification on me when they pulled my body out of the alley. (Matt would later joke that they had probably picked that name because they figured I was a dead fish.) I suppose I could have been.

I have spent the past few days, when I allow myself to think about what happened, wondering why I did regain consciousness.

I have been thinking, which I accept you won't find comforting, that it would have been better if I had not. Another hour and all my problems, my exhaustion with life, would have ended. I was unconscious, after all, and thus not in any pain. Body and soul would simply have separated, at long last, and this long ordeal would have ceased.

But I did regain consciousness. I found myself in a pool of my own blood at the foot of the rickety stairs leading up to my flat. I had busted open the back of my head on the concrete there and lay bleeding for hours--maybe five or six is my estimate.

My blood loss was such that I was too weak to get to my feet. I called out for help for a long time, but no one heard me.

I decided to crawl over to the fence separating the property my building is on from the house I worked on next door. I would use the fence to pull myself to my feet. My plan was to pull myself along the fence toward the street where I hoped someone would call an ambulance.

I fell.

Too weak to keep my knees from buckling, even with the support of the fence, I crawled along the alleyway between the two houses. I continued to call for help as I crawled along the alleyway.

A neighbor finally heard me, looked out her window, then came to her balcony and saw all the blood. She freaked and had her roommate call 911. I lost consciousness again shortly after the EMTs arrived. Unknown Mackerel.

When I awakened again in the Trauma Unit, the heads of doctors in masks filling my field of vision like out of some movie, I overhead that my blood pressure was now "up to" 60 over 40. From my own experience, working in a mental hospital Admissions ward during my youth, I knew that was dangerously low. I was freezing, too. I knew they had some type of heating blanket tossed over multiple sheets on me, but I was colder than I'd ever felt. Death was so near, I thought. But the doctors were fighting to keep death away. They were asking me who I was and who they could call about me.

Did I know what day it was? Of course. Thursday the 25th. Yesterday was my fifty-second birthday. Did I know where I was? Charity Hospital in New Orleans, I supposed. Good. Good. Just stay with us. You're going to make it.

I was freezing. I was in and out of both consciousness and attentiveness. They would do what they had to do I knew. Catheters, transfusions, CAT scans, X-rays. I was freezing. It was all happening somewhere outside of my concern. I was on some conveyor belt of events over which I had no control. They would do what they had to do and I was theirs until it was over.

As happens every time I visit the hospital, a new area of concern was found. When all the other doctors had finished their work, we all had to wait on the verdict of the urologist. It seems that, this time, there was a problem with one of my kidneys. A couple of scars. I had to agree to come back in a couple months so that they could test again and make sure there was not cancer there.

I knew that I was out of the woods when they finally took the cuff off my neck. The X-rays looked good, I was told; my neck was not broken. A doctor asked that I move my head and neck around for him. I had not been allowed to move my neck for hours. Another doctor said that there appeared to be no bleeding in the brain.

Matt and Jo decided that I should stay at their place for the first day out of the hospital, concerned that complications might emerge. Jo said something about people with head injuries needing to be observed for a day or so. The "Wound Care" fact sheet the hospital gave me upon release said much the same thing.

"If anything happened to you," Jo told me, "who would know? How would you get help?"

Matt told me, the morning after my release from hospital, that the person who they had as Patient Liaison for Charity Hospital had been quite impressive. She was very calming, he said. While not revealing any information which might lead to alarming conclusions, she had left him feeling informed. He said he had worried when the most she would commit to was that my condition was "guarded." But, he continued, she made sure that he did not worry that all was lost.

I told him that morning that I was not at all convinced that having survived was a positive development. I would have to think about it for another couple of days…

I think lots of the people who lived in New Orleans, especially the kinds of people who moved to New Orleans, got overstimulated by its atmosphere of sex and death. I can't imagine them--us--living anywhere else for very long. Especially not in the Protestant, festival-barren, unerotic real America of strip malls and "Last Calls."

But I know one thing: I just about died and then I came back.

After Katrina, I watched New Orleans just about die and now I am watching my brutal mistress come back, too.

We're both getting ready for the next round.

THE "NEW" NEW ORLEANS

My friend Mputhumi Ntabeni, who lives in South Africa, watched the aftermath of Hurricane Katrina on CNN, as did many around the world, and tried to make sense of the images he was seeing. This couldn't be America he was looking at, he felt. Trying to make sense of the images and the horrors he saw, he contacted a colleague who taught at Xavier University of Louisiana in New Orleans, Nicole Pepinster Greene, who is Associate Professor, Department of English. This is what she wrote back to him:

As we sat watching these images of the thousands of displaced and suffering black people at the Superdome and Convention Centre, a commentator remarked: "They're looking as if they're coming from some place else ... this just isn't America." These scenes conjured up another New Orleans landmark, Congo Square, where Africans used to await sale and transportation as slaves.

But this is America today and this is another diaspora. A black doctor treating young African Americans who had walked 130 miles from New Orleans said their feet resembled those of runaway slaves. People who had never left their neighbourhoods before are being forcibly moved to other towns and other states: Texas, Arkansas, Iowa, West Virginia. This "some place else" they are arriving from is unfamiliar not only to the rest of the world, but to many Americans. It is the New Orleans most do not know; the New Orleans that is 66 per cent African-American; the New Orleans where one third of the people, black and white, live below the poverty line; the New Orleans that has always stayed behind; the New Orleans that has all but been abandoned.

Will New Orleans remain? The centre has held: the French Quarter, the central business district, the warehouse district, the garden district, Audubon Park and Zoo, uptown, the universities and medical centres, among them Loyola, Tulane, Xavier. Entrepreneurs will prosper, and the middle classes will rebuild. Musicians have already vowed to return to the city that we love. But without its people, New Orleans will be an unimaginably different city. As I write, a thousand bodies are being identified and Mayor Nagin predicts thousands more will be found. Hundreds are still trapped. And having lost everything, this population will not be able to return without huge efforts.

Xavier University of Lousiana is located directly in the front of the now-famous 17th Street Canal in New Orleans. It sustained significant wind and flood damage and now much its future lies in question. Due to a FEMA ruling approved by the Congress five years, Xavier—like other private and non-profit institutions—is inevitable to receive any funding from that agency to repair flood damage. This is significant for a number of reasons. Xavier is the oldest traditionally Black Catholic university in the United States. It is known for producing the highest percentage of Black doctors from its undergraduate program of any single institution in the country and is a corner of heatlh care in New Orleans. In addition, a full 75% of the Black pharmacists in the United States today are Xavier graduates.

Considering this stunning record of achievement, you would expect that Xavier would be among those institutions in New Orleans guaranteed to be saved. If you did, your expectations would be wrong.

Immediately after Katrina, Xavier--in an effort to remain viable— submitted a proposal to the Department of Education asking that it institute its summer break during the months of September, October and November in order to buy time for clean-up and reconstruction and allow its students to gain the full year of education they expected. Both Tulane and Loyola Universities in New Orleans offered to provide classes free of charge for those Xavier students who wished to take them while awaiting their own school's re-opening.

On September 2, 2005, the Department of Education issued a ruling that stated that Xavier students and those of other private and non-profit institutions from the region affected by Katrina would only be provided the financial aid they had already been approved to receive if they took courses at universities, including state schools, that had not been affected by the disaster. When one considers the financial status of most Black students, this was a significant ruling. When one considers the future of Xavier University of Louisiana, the future of another historically Black university in brought into question.

There are many signs that this part of the New Orleans we have lost, won't be the same again.

Both Xavier and Dillard, the other Black college in New Orleans, were on low ground. Both were near canals.

It has been said about New Orleans that it is a city where you could find a bar and a church every block and a half. If you lived in New Orleans when I did, at the beginning of the twenty-first century, you knew that was almost true. Our lives were centered around these two institutions. That led one of my fellow bartenders, Jolie at Mollly's at the Market, to once proclaim that being a bartender in New Orleans was like being a rock star anywhere else.

Those of us there at the top of service worker food chain had, per force, to deal with the bar owners of New Orleans, mad people to a one.

One of the most renowned bar owners in the French Quarter was Jim Monaghan, Sr., owner of Molly's at the Market, so named because it was near the end of the French Market tourist trap of our town. Molly's was the locus of the lives of many of us in French Quarter, by design. It was a "decent" bar at the center of our daily drama and debauchery, a place that we could pretend to be like the rest of the people in America. And the grand poobah of that time in the city of New Orleans, was Jim Monaghan, Sr. After him, Jim Monaghan, Jr., stepped into place and assumed the throne. We dutifully did obeisance, though some of us denigrated the latter.

Not me. Jim Monaghan, Jr., was and is my friend. We had the tie of both having lived in Colorado before living in New Orleans.

Among the thirty bars owned by Jim Sr., at one time or the other, outright or as a partner, in New Orleans were Bonaparte's Retreat, Burgundy Street Outback, Katy's Underground, (he owned The Abbey several times), Mollys on Toulouse, Nick's Place, Erin Rose, The Patio, and Easy Eddie's. (Thanks and a tip of the hat to my pal, Tim Farley, long-time manager of Molly's at he Market, for an assist on this list.)

Figure 14. Exterior of Molly's at the Market on St. Patrick's--the "window" where many of us would sit. Courtesy of Tim Farley.

I have already said that anybody who was anybody in New Orleans politics was a Guest Bartender at Molly's at the Market if they wanted to get elected. Molly's will always be part of New Orleans and the

French Quarter. I've already reported that it is open as I write this love story of the city that is lost.

Molly's will be part of the "new" New Orleans I understand our government is planning, and it will infect that New Orleans with the disease of lust, sex and death that was such a vital part of our old city. I guaran-damn-tee it.

Thinking of the Monaghan family, not only both Jims, but also Alana, Jim Jr,'s wife, his children, Tierney and Jim III – who we all knew as "Tres" (pronounced "Tray,") it seems fitting that this last chapter of this book about New Orleans should be chapter thirteen.

The last Monaghan bar opened in New Orleans, on Frenchmen Street, only a block up from The Spotted Cat, was Monaghan's 13. Tim Farley, the manager of Molly's at the Market, was also manager of that bar. (See Appendix: Voices from The Storm)

Thirteen is a special number for the Monaghan's of New Orleans and for me.

Jim Monaghan Sr. passed from this world on December 13, 2001, only months after I moved to New Orleans, but I was honored to be one of the many people of our city to be invited to take part in his Second Line. Mr. Monaghan was born on May 13, 1938.

Andre Codrescu--the National Public Radio commentator, publisher of the Exquisite Corpse Web site and one of my customers at The Spotted Cat--wrote Mr. Monaghan's obituary for the Gambit Weekly. Part of what Mr. Codrescu wrote was this:

A publican of the first order, Jim owned more Quarter bars than most people visit, but was best known at Molly's. A complex creature who was even loudly criticized by those who loved him best and continued to be loved by a majority of countless girlfriends and four wives. The last wife, Liz, said to be careful that any of Jim's generosity not be taken as weakness, "so if you have to be nice, do it abrasively."

It was a well-known fact of the Monaghan regime, the place we made our favorite watering hole and the center of our lives, that he rotated bartenders on a regular basis. You could always depend on there being (mostly) cute women behind the bar who were well-endowed. You could always depend on most of your friends who worked at a Monaghan bar to eventually be fired, "rotated out," in favor of new blood. Jolie was a survivor, on that count.

Curtis managed to avoid one bullet by being shifted from Molly's at the Market to the Erin Rose. But, ultimately, he had to go. Jak got 86'ed from the bar but continued to be a bartender. The stories go on and on about the Monaghan bars.

At the back of Molly's, the back bar on your way to the toilet facilities, there is a mural of long-running patrons. My pal Scott Salin is on the mural, as is Mary McGinn and other French Quarter denizens who were part of my life in The New Orleans That Was Lost.

I think of all this, all this that was part of wonder of my life in New Orleans, as I pick a copy of USA Today and read about what the Powers That Be plan to do for (to) my lost city as they rebuild her.

New Orleans' pulse was 60 over 40 after Katrina. I, of all her citizens, can relate to that. And what do I read they mean to do to bring her back?

I hear that Newt Gingrich, the former Speaker of the House, has already jumped into the fray, suggesting that New Orleans end up being more like a Disneyland for adults.

I was compelled to read the USA TODAY story " Dreams are emerging of a 'new' New Orleans" by Richard Willig, originally posted on their Web site on 13 September and updated on the 14th. Here's part of what that gentleman said:

… As the shock of one of America's worst natural disaster wears off and floodwaters are pumped out of New Orleans, public figures from local performers to President Bush are beginning to speak of reviving the 287-year-old city as if such a thing is inevitable.

Figure 15. The Zulu Parade at Mardi Gras 2005.

They are contemplating what urban planner Robert Lang of Virginia Tech says has "never been done before in America": Using what could be hundreds of billions of public and private dollars to rebuild a modern city on a scale far beyond what happened in San Francisco after its 1906 earthquake, or in Chicago after its 1871 fire.

But what kind of city will rise from the receding waters, and when, and how?

Rebuilding is a complex issue, layered with racially sensitive questions about how to revamp the city while luring back the blue-collar and low-income residents — most of them black — who made up the bulk of the roughly half-million evacuees from the area who now are scattered across America. At stake is how much of New Orleans' identity — its unique combination of grit and refinement, bawdiness and charm — will be washed away for good.

Politicians, urban planners, business leaders and local residents with different views of a "new" New Orleans already are campaigning for their competing visions.

U.S. Rep. William Jefferson, D-La., whose New Orleans home was flooded, would focus on creating a city where tax credits, housing subsidies and jobs programs would be used to encourage the return of its working class.

U.S. Rep. Bobby Jindal, R-La., whose home in nearby Kenner also was damaged, would appoint a rebuilding czar and dust off plans to diversify the city's industrial base and modernize its hospitals and public housing.

Scientists such as John Rennie, editor of Scientific American, are talking about a safer and perhaps smaller city in which wetlands would be expanded to protect against storms.

Singer Art Neville of the Neville Brothers is calling for a "Newer Orleans" — a city re-populated by returning evacuees and protected by a new set of the "best levees ever built."

And Dane Ciolino, a criminal defense lawyer and a law professor at the University of New Orleans, wants a rebuilt city that excludes the "looters and the shooters" but that remains racially and economically diverse. He fears that restoring only the upper-income residential areas such as the Garden District and the tourist sites of the French Quarter — the areas in New Orleans least damaged by the flooding — would turn the city into an "adult Disneyland with cocktails."

Reading this, I'm thinking: Oh, dang! What about letting those of us who lived and loved in New Orleans come back and rebuild it and make it back into OUR city. Barbary Coast or ashram? Do you care what we think?

Maybe not.

We're not politically important, we don't have a lot of money, we don't contribute to political campaigns for people who don't have our interests at heart and – hell! – too many of us our Black anyway.

I'd surely like to live in a city built by a scientist or politician or criminal defense lawyer more than I would one built by average working people. (That was sarcasm.)

I've been waiting to be socially-engineered MY WHOLE DAMNED LIFE. How 'bout you?

My former co-worker, Tanya, who was a home-owner in the Lower Nine—as many people in that part of the Parish were—whose home was near the border with St. Bernard Parish, has not been able to assess the name to her house. She is living in the shelter in Gonzales, LA, for now.

When I was finally able to contact her, it was to learn that Tanya had spent the week in Washington, D.C., lobbying the Congress not to forget the people of the Ninth Ward when considering the rebuilding of New Orleans. She could speak from the heart because she has lived there all of her life and simply wants to go back home. She has heard the rumors about declaring Eminent Domain and simply bull-dozing the Lower Nine in its entirety. She prays, for herself and her family, that that will not happen.

You shall either take the facts and history of the lost city of New Orleans, the city I knew and loved, to heart and make sure that it doesn't become "Disneyland with cocktails" or you will decide that we were all overly romantic, overly melodramatic and not enough like you to be worth salvaging.

You will say that that the New Orleans that loved me, jailed me, almost killed me --even while I kept loving her--is wrong explicitly because she was not America as you know it. But you will be wrong. New Orleans was only unique, spiritually, for America, because she exemplified the idea of personal freedom. She was a libertarian's dream. America is about sex and death, too. Admit it.

Figure 16. A painter at Jackson Square.

Look at your advertisements for automobiles, perfume and clothing and tell me that you are not just the sanitized version of what we put on the street corners of New Orleans. Bourbon Street was just a reflection of the commercial urge made Protestant in the Great American Mall.

I don't know what the "new" New Orleans will be like. I hear that people like the Heritage Foundation have been talking to the Bush Administration about making New Orleans an experiment for their hyper-capitalist theories like they are doing in Iraq.

I hear that at least one Louisiana plutocrat has said that he's going to do all he can to make sure that no poor people and no Black people--like those of us who lived in the Lower Nine--will ever come back to the "new" New Orleans.

I don't know. These could just be urban legends.

Either way, you must know that I'll go back to New Orleans, one day, when I can. As every writer knows, the stories never end.

APPENDIX: Voices from The Storm

VOICES FROM THE STORM
THE AFTERMATH INTERVIEWS

LIZARD LICK, 13 September, 2005

TIM FARLEY is a thirty-four year old bar manager and bartender who lived in the Marigny district of New Orleans until Sunday, 28 August, 2005. During the week of 12 September, he was interviewed by various media outlets because he had been manager of a locus of life in the French Quarter, Molly's at the Market, as well of the new Monaghan venture on Frenchmen Street, Monaghan's 13.

 I assumed, after receiving a telephone call from Molly's over the weekend and discovering that it was again open for business, that Tim must still be in New Orleans. Now that cell phone access was re-appearing for area code 504, I decided to try reaching Tim on his cell phone. He was in a meeting with a group of community organizations that wanted to set up a fundraising and relief effort for the service workers of New Orleans.

The meeting was being held in Milwaukee, Wisconsin.

Tim had been a friend for a number of years. We'd shared morning coffees together, either when he was a customer at my bar or I was a customer at his. We'd also had few beers or Crown Royals together. When his wife was pregnant with their son Javin, Lisa had stopped into The Spotted Cat to grab a water and chat--only minutes before her water broke. Their son always seemed to have a special sparkle in his eyes--those amazing eyes!--whenever I met him and seemed to flash me a knowing smile.

Tim and I spoke that evening.

ROD: First of all, how are you doing?

TIM: I'm all right. I've been busy trying to get housing for my family. I just got back from picking up a fixture to fix my mother-in-law's toilet.

ROD: When did you get out?

TIM: The Sunday before. We left at 3 a.m. We stayed at the Motel 6 in Memphis and watched most of what happened on television from our hotel. I laughed on the way, telling Javin we were going to Graceland to see Elvis.

ROD: Man, he can understand Elvis now? How long has it been?

TIM: He's three now. I know, "Time flies."

ROD: Don't remind me! So before I get "formal" on you, I do want to ask you one thing. Just for my sense of things. You said you've been doing lots of interviews. What kind of questions are the mainstream folks asking these days?

TIM: I lot of them start by asking when I got out. I tell them how upsetting it is for me to watch some of the coverage that's being going on because they act like people are surprised this would happen. I wasn't surprised! I don't know anyone from New Orleans who was surprised. Everybody knew that we got a Category 3 or above it was time to leave. And that's the other thing. I let know that we're upset about how some people claim that those people from New Orleans were "too stubborn to leave." I don't believe they can say that!. People didn't stay because they were stubborn, they stayed because they can't afford to leave.

As far as I'm concerned, only The Onion got it right. Did you see their headline: "White Foragers Fearful of Black Looters."

ROD: So what's it been like since you left?

TIM: Well, like I said, I've been looking for a house here. I think we'll have the place by next weekend. The people who are there now are supposed to be moving out by next weekend.

The toughest part is when Javin says, "I wannah go home." How can I tell my son that we can't go back? I try to explain to him that we're going to be here for a while longer for now.

ROD: Well, if and when they get New Orleans cleaned up and back on her feet, would you go back to New Orleans?

TIM: Hell, I'd love to be there right now. I mean, I put all those years into building a life there. I didn't work that long and that hard just to walk away from it. But I have a son. New Orleans is no place to raise a child right now. Being there would not make a good parent. My son needs schools, parks, a zoo, an aquarium. I can't take the risk of what would happen to his future if we lived in New Orleans.

ROD: How long did you live in New Orleans?

TIM: Eight years. I'm originally from Cleveland.

ROD: Why did you go to New Orleans?

TIM: I'd never been there. Once I got there I said, "This is Home." So I went back to Cleveland, quit my job, broke up with my girlfriend, sold my car, and moved down to New Orleans.

ROD: How did you become Manager of Molly's?

TIM: I was working on Bourbon Street at what was then Patou's Cajun Cabin. It's not Patou's anymore but there's still a Cajun Cabin. Anyway, I knew about Molly's because just about all my friends had been fired from there. [Laughs.] I was drinking at the Hideout [on Decatur Street. The establishment is now called Aunt Tiki's]--during the day, of course. So when I decided to go home on my bike, I realized I was too drunk for being on a motor vehicle, so I decided to park it in front of Molly's. Jim [Monaghan Sr.] was sitting in the front window. So I yelled out, "Hey, Asshole, when are you going to fire all those losers and give me a job?"

"Come see me tomorrow!" he shot back.

So I did. Been there ever since.

ROD: Where did you live in New Orleans.

TIM: I've always lived in the Quarter or the Marigny. Well, there one was very brief stint in MidCity but mostly it was either the Quarter or the Marigny.

ROD: I think when we met you were living in the Quarter. Why live in the French Quarter?

TIM: Because it's nonstop. There's just this non-stop activity in the Quarter and I loved that.

ROD: What made you move to the Marigny?

TIM: Well, it was a lot cheaper for the space we need. I mean, after we had the baby, there was no way Lisa was going to have us living above a bar. We had to get a house.

ROD: I always thought of you as a fixture of the Quarter but it doesn't sound like you're going back.

TIM: I can't. The environmental degradation alone is a big factor.

ROD: Did you hear Mayor Nagin declared that the Quarter was safe this afternoon? [13 September]

TIM: Yeah but I won't risk my son's life on that. Besides, raising a child you need more than clean water. You need hospitals, schools, playgrounds, and like I told you zoos and aquariums.

ROD: I hear you. Thanks for talking to me. Let's stay in touch. And kiss Lisa for me.

LIZARD LICK, 16 September, 2005

TY WATFORD is a 40 year old carpenter and artist who has lived in the French Quarter for fifteen years. He shares his apartment with his partner, Ashley, who is now a bartender at Molly's at the Market. They live on Dumaine Street in the Quarter.

Ty started a business, three years ago, delivering fine art and delicate antiques to the galleries and businesses that festoon Royal Street and its environs. This year, 2005, was the first profitable year for his new business. "But I wasn't just working for the money," Ty told me, when I called him at Molly's at the Market, one of few land lines that is up in New Orleans today, to conduct this interview. "I also want to make sure that the job is right for my clients.

"Here in New Orleans, as I know you know, a lot of it is all about trust."

ROD: Okay, you stayed in the Quarter, through all of this. What has it been like?

TY: What do you think? When our neighbors left before the storm, they all started leaving food and water in front of our door because they knew we meant to ride the storm out. That helped.

Ashley and I were sitting on our balcony when Katrina came in and we watched the balcony across the street on that building just go away.

At two in the afternoon on Monday, when it was still windy but not that dangerous, we made our first walk through the Quarter just to see how much damage had really been done.

On Tuesday, we could see that there was mostly just some wind damage. Tree branches down, that kind of thing. That was Tuesday and Wednesday. I think it was Wednesday we brought out our brooms to start cleaning up. Our other friends that stayed, we got in touch with them, and we all started to do the same.

Let me tell you something, Rod. Among this group of friends here in the Quarter, everybody's needs were met. We shared food, water, everything. I think you'll like this. We decided as part of our clean-up krewe we would all wear these red shirts while we were sweepin' up. If somebody had a red shirt with something written on it, they turned it inside out. [Laughs.]

Figure 17. A Garden District House.

ROD: Let's back up. Why did you move to New Orleans in the first place, Ty?

TY: I'm a carpenter by training but an artist at heart. I always wanted to restore great architecture and New Orleans seemed like the place to me. I grew up in Hattiesburg, Mississippi, and had always heard about the restoration work in New Orleans. For me it was like restoring great pieces of art.

Ashley's from Hattiesburg, too. I went back there seven years ago and we hooked up and she moved back here to start a fine art framing business.

ROD: How are things there now?

TY: It's comin' back slowly. There's electricity in about eight blocks of the CBD [Central Business District] but that's about it.

ROD: Damn. So you can't get much news or information, can you?

TY: We don' want it. Even at places with a generator, I don't want to listen to the radio. Frankly, most of us here in the Quarter just don't care what ya'll think outside of New Orleans. We're here and we mean to stay.

And you know what? We love Mayor Nagin and we think he's great.

ROD: Meaning, you've heard from other journalists like me that Ray is takin' a hit outside of Nawlins?

TY: We don't care. He stayed here and did his job.

ROD: More outside perspective: I hear some people, who are paranoid, are sneaking into the New Orleans through the back roads and other people are just driving right in and getting waved through the checkpoints. What can you tell me about that?

TY: I'll tell you somethin'. Some folks here are even generatin' their own Press passes to be able to move around the city. I know somebody who took the logo from a National Geographic and used that. They just laminate that over their ID, maybe take a backstage pass from a concert and put it in that sleeve, then hang that around their neck and they're good to go. Even the Blackwater Security mercenaries get fooled by that. I understand the smart ones bring a camera with 'em to look like Press, too.

ROD: I'll pretend that I'm surprised.

So listen, DemocracyNow! Is reporting that prisoners from OPP [Orleans Parish Prison] are being held at the Greyhound/Amtrak terminal in the CBD. I've been trying to get a confirmation. Do you know anything about that?

TY: I've heard that from a couple of people. I've met a couple of people who had photos of prisoners being booked at the terminal but I can't tell you whether they are being held there or not, Rod. What I do know is that there's a rumor that that is where people who are being picked up are being shipped from.

ROD: Are you listening to the news about the country's plans for rebuilding Nawlins?

TY: Most of the people in the French Quarter don't care, Rod. You used to live here, right? You know.

We don't listen to the radio on purpose. We know that it's more than a spot. It's important.

And while I'm at it, let me tell you something else. Jim Monaghan? If this situation had really gotten worse, he would have been like a warlord down here. The good people are just drawn to him and the bad people fear him. That is why Molly's is open every day and serving customers right now.

ROD: Well, Jim and I are friends.

TY: I know. That's why he's letting me use this phone for the interview. Listen, I don't know if you want to publish this in your book or not but things are still very different down here. I ran into some kids trying to get to Indiana after being harassed by some of the martial law folks down here, the cops, and I had this Volvo that I just gave them to get home, right?

Well, I was talkin' to some guys who were bringin' ambulances in for here and they heard the story. Well, you know what, I have an ambulance that I drive around now.

Can you print that kind of thing?

ROD: Ty, it's still America, as far as I know ... But maybe I'm just thinking like Snake Plitkin.

[We both laugh.]

Look, man, thanks for taking the time to talk to me, okay! Tell Jim I said Hi and to say Hi to Alana for me, okay?

TY: Call back if you need anything before you finish the book. We get autographed copies, right?

ROD: As long as you pick them up at Molly's. Thanks, man.

LIZARD LICK, 26 September, 2005: Food; I haven't said much about food in this book, which is surprising when the topic is New Orleans. One reason for that is that on my budget there were not a lot of dinners at Galitoire's on the agenda. Red beans and rice, or the free Saturday and Sunday afternoon barbecue feasts at The Abbey were more my style. Getting invited to a crawfish boil (the latter word pronounced "berl" by many a New Orleanian) was a high point of a good week for me. Splitting one of the wonderful, huge barbecued brisket sandwiches from Tujac's on Decatur with my pal Scott, while we sat at Molly's around lunch time, was a veritable feast.

So, I decided to defer to GREG COWMAN, whose uncle the chef Tom Cowman was an icon of New Orleans fare, to help me fill in the blanks. Greg's book, Secrets of a New Orleans, Recipes from Tom Cowman's Cookbook (University Press of Mississippi, 1999) features not only many of the dishes Tom Cowman made famous at Restaurant Jonathan and the Upperline but also tales from Tom's career. If you were in New Orleans in the late 1970s and early 1980s, it was difficult to miss the billboards featuring Tom Cowman's smiling face.

Greg lived in MidCity and worked at the historic Napoleon House in the French Quarter before Katrina. When I caught up with Greg, he was in Abita Springs, LA, (north of Lake Pontchartrain) where he has been staying with friends since the first hurricane, Katrina, hit New Orleans.

ROD: I figured you were the best person I could talk to about food.

GREG: I'm not sure that's true. I simply wrote about what Tom showed me and what I learned to love about New Orleans cuisine. He was the real magician, the real star.

And I don't know if you heard this already or not, but they're saying that nearly 25% of the restaurants in New Orleans are either severely damaged or totally destroyed.

ROD: I hadn't. That's a real tragedy for a city known for its food.

GREG: Yeah. I believe the Napoleon House will still be there, since we were on high ground, but you gottah wonder about some of the other places.

ROD: Let's start with some background. Give me a brief overview of where your uncle was chef in New Orleans and why he came to prominence.

GREG: I suppose he's most famous now for his time at the Upperline, uptown, where he was chef from about '87 – 94. They got consistent four star ratings from the Times-Picayune while Tom was there. Before that he did a brief stint, around, again earning the Times-Picayune four beans. But he started, and made the name for himself, at Restaurant Jonathan—where the Funky Butt is now, or was, I guess I should say—on Ramparts. That was from 1974-86. Again, four beans.

I guess what made Tom so celebrated was that he used an imagination and flare that you couldn't find any place other than New Orleans in those days. He was a visionary, one of the first New Orleans chets to move away from the usual etoufes and gumbos, the creole cooking that you would get anywhere. What made him shine was bringing in the influences of Mexico, Thailand and places like that and blending them with the spices, the herbs, the seafood you can get in New Orleans in exciting ways. That was Gene Bourg had to say about him.

ROD: Gene Bourg, the Food critic at the Times-Picayune?

GREG: Yes. He did the foreword for the book of Tom's recipe. He was a great fan.

ROD: Nowadays, of course, we get much the same thing from other famous chefs associated with New Orleans. Emeril LeGasse immediately comes to mind.

GREG: You're right. But I think Tom was one of the first.

ROD: Why New Orleans, one has to ask. What was it about the atmosphere in New Orleans that made for the marriage between Tom's style and New Orleans cuisine?

GREG: That's easy! You have fresh seafood year-round in New Orleans. You've got a twelve month growing season for your herbs and spices. Tom used to say that that was the problem with attempting to offer this kind of cooking anywhere else—if you're somewhere else, like St. Paul, you can't get your ingredients year-round.

ROD: Okay, if people reading this book want to get their mitts on Tom's recipes where can they order the book?

GREG: The usual places. But for you, if you give them my e-mail address, I'll send them an autographed copy and give them a discount price if they say they came from you.

ROD: Thanks! That's kind of you.

TO ORDER Secrets of a New Orleans Chef, Recipes from Tom Cowman's Cookbook by Greg Cowman, send an e-mail to gcowman@east.cox.net.

LIZARD LICK, 28 September 2005

KATY RECKDAHL moved to New Orleans in 1999 to spend a year working as a producer on the National Public Radio program "American Routes." As she tells it, she fell in love with the city and with a horn player (Mervin "Kid Merv" Campbell) and remained there until after Hurricane Katrina hit. In fact, short before Katrina made landfall, Katy was in Touro Hospital giving birth to her first son.

While working for public radio, Katy was also freelancing for various newspapers and eventually landed a job as a stringer for the New York Times and a steady berth with the Gambit Weekly. At the Gambit Weekly throughout her time in New Orleans, she focused on articles about issues of social justice. That's how we met. You couldn't go to a Second Line anywhere in New Orleans where Katy was not known by most of the musicians, she had friends in other communities, as well, because of her reporting.

Before moving to New Orleans, she had been a staff writer for the City Paper in Minneapolis, MN. This is what she wrote for Mike Mosedale's blog at that paper:

All day Saturday, people were getting ready to evacuate. Everyone you saw in the street would say, "Are you leaving?" Among our friends, it was 50-50 between people staying, people going. We were debating because I was so enormously pregnant--38 weeks along, big as a house and four centimeters dilated, which meant I could go on to labor at any moment.

Last year, I had evacuated for Hurricane Ivan. We spent 14 hours on the road, and then we got two drops of rain in New Orleans. I knew I couldn't do that this time. For one thing, you really don't own your bladder at that point in pregnancy. And if I had gone into labor, I probably would been forced to give birth in a car.

At about 10 p.m., when Merv got home from his gig, my contractions were getting pretty close. So he borrowed a car and drove like a speed demon to Touro--me in the back seat, on all fours and in a lot of pain.

When we arrived to the hospital, they discovered Hector was lying sideways, so they had to turn him about 90 degrees before he could come out. I could have never given birth to him in a car. It turned out we probably did the right thing by staying.

I started to push at midnight. Hector wasn't born until 4:14 in the morning. He was a cute, mellow little dude and we called some people to say that we were staying and then I fell asleep. About eight hours after I gave birth, the hospital was put on lock down, which meant no one could leave and no one could enter. So after that, I really didn't think again about evacuating.

About 6 a.m. on Monday morning, we were awakened by the head nurse. The hurricane came through--it sounded like a train--and she was telling everyone to move in the hallways. Originally, they had thought we would be okay in our rooms because the glass was rated for 200 mph winds. But after a few windows broke in the upper stories, someone decided all the patients would sit out the hurricane in the hallways.

We were on generator power all through the hurricane. Initially, the phones were still working. The girl across from me was talking to her mom, who lives in the lower ninth ward--one of the places that was hit really badly. Her mom was saying she was in the attic, trying to get onto the roof. Then the line went dead. All through the morning, there was this horrible pall on our floor because we realized that her mom could be dead.

The generator for our part of the hospital failed around 7 o'clock that night and we left were in total darkness. It was bizarre to live that way, no electricity for two days, then no water. We were using the light of the cellphone to get around the room at night, and to light up my nipples. It was so crazy. Merv would be standing there with an open cell phone, pointed at my nipple, and we'd try to get the baby to latch on.

We started to get reports on an A.M. radio call-in show, which was the only outside communication we had. They said that the ninth ward had been hit pretty bad and that a lot of people had probably died. But then we were also hearing that the rest of the city had survived. It seemed like it was just a matter of getting the power back on, cleaning up and helping people in the ninth ward. So we felt really lucky, like everything could be back to normal in a few days.

Then on Tuesday, we started hearing a lot of really dismal news. We were hearing about houses completely under water in other parts of the city. We were hearing about the water flowing toward Uptown. A nurse came in and said her house was under water. It sounded like some of the places really near our house were completely under water, too. We heard that the neighborhood right next to us, the St. Bernard/seventh ward area, had been pretty badly hit and that this store called Circle Foods had water up to its arches. So Merv and I started to realize, "Oh, shit, our place might be under water too."

Katy, Merv and Hector was driven to an airport in Baton Rouge by one of the nurses from Touro that following Thursday. From there, they initially went to stay with her sister in Tempe, AZ. When I caught up with her, they were staying in a hotel in Chandler, AZ, where they had recently been joined by members of the Treme Brass Band, with whom Merv plays.

ROD: One thing that didn't come out in either your piece for Mike Mosedale's blog on your subsequent article for the (Minneapolis) Star Tribune ("Ex-Minnesotan gives birth when Katrina strikes" September 10, 2005) was whether or not you and Kid believe you'll return to New Orleans. How about that?

KATY: We don't know. It depends on when it opens up. I mean, my job is gone. The Gambit is completely washed away.

ROD: And Merv? I mean, he is touring quite a bit. Does he feel any ties to New Orleans?

KATY: Even, in exile, we're tied to the New Orleans music community—New Orleans traditional jazz, which is what Merv plays. If it's possible, we'd go back.

The thing is, our landlord called yesterday to find out what we are going to do. Even though we don't have that great an apartment, it is in the French Quarter, off Ramparts, which means its dry and there's going to be plumbing soon. So—you won't believe this, he wants to give us a week to decide what we're going to do. We tried to explain that with a new baby it's just not that easy to keep moving around but it sounded like he felt he could make something off the place with people looking for high ground and we were just a burden for him.

ROD: Nice guy.

KATY: Well, we'll give it a week and see what's it's like. If he won't be nice, then I guess I'll have to be a little not nice, too…

ROD: Most of your articles for the Gambit Weekly dealt with issues of social justice. What's your take on those kinds of topics now from what you know about post-Katrina New Orleans?

KATY: I see the a lot of the same problems, really. The same stories, only with different people perpetrating them. What I was covering was basically local authorities screwing the little guys. Well, I did do that story covering Medicare, but most what I wrote about was local. No its federal.

ROD: You've probably heard about the OPP (Orleans Parish Prison) story, right? The inmates in Templeman III being left in chest-high water with no Deputies around and no way to get out? Human Rights Watch said this week that there are over 500 people unaccounted for.

KATY: Yeah, I've heard about that and, again, there's no surprise. Louisiana has an unhealthy attitude about putting people away for minor infraction, that was there from before, so I don't see that the people at OPP would get treated any better than the average, poor people on the street.

ROD: In your City Paper piece, you address the question, "Why didn't people leave?"—Well, Mike does in his intro. But the other question, of the New Orleans we knew, was why people stayed. You said you fell in love with New Orleans. What was it about the city that you loved?

KATY: It's a sweet city, New Orleans is.

ROD: Can you be more specific? "Sweet," how?

KATY: Well, for example, any time you're walking down the street
you could have somebody come up to you with a ridiculous story, or
someone would just stop and say something that made you both
giggle, or a band would be going by, or you'd see something dressed
really unusually. There was always something entertaining going on in
New Orleans, just walking down the street.

And there was another kind of sweetness that I think people were just
raised to have in New Orleans. Someone might tell you your hair
looked nice today, and they wouldn't be hitting on you. Or you drop
your sweater and a kid in baggie pants down around his butt would
call out, "Hey, lady, you dropped your sweater" and go pick it up for
you, something someone who looks like that is not supposed to do.

Jut a basic sweetness. People are raised to be nice to each other in a
way you don't find anyplace else.

And, of course, you've got the added benefits of a very artistic
atmosphere. But it was that day-to-day stuff that made me fall in love
with New Orleans.

ROD: What else do you miss? What do you wish I'd asked you?

KATY: Well, the hardest part is going through this pregnancy not
being in New Orleans. I mean, the whole time I was there people were
making me food, asking if I was sure I could keep riding my bike
around, touching me to see if Hector was kicking or moving around to
the music. I felt more part of a community.

I know people are trying to keep that community feeling going on the
phone, but it's not the same. I miss having people around, aunties and
uncles fussing over the baby, passing him around, that kind of thing
that you can't get over a telephone and miles away. That's the hardest
part right now.

Figure 18: A "doorfront" sign in New Orleans immediately after Katrina.